Getting into psychology courses

D1381922

PW

Senior Library

TORMEAD LIBRARY
This book is the property of
TORMEAD SCHOOL.

Please make sure you have issued the book
correctly to yourself on the library computer,
or signed it out on the blue sheet.

Loan period
The book is due back three weeks after you
borrowed it, or earlier if you have finished
with it.

Renewals
The librarian will renew the book on request if
no one else has reserved it.

Please take care of this book. You will be
asked to pay for any loss or damage.

WITHDRAWN

Getting into

Psychology Courses

Getting into guides

Getting into

Psychology Courses

Jody-Helena Williams

12th edition

Getting into Psychology Courses

This 12th edition published in 2018 by Trotman Education, an imprint of Crimson Publishing, 21d Charles Street, Bath BA1 1HX.

© Crimson Publishing Ltd 2018

Author: Jody-Helena Williams

11th edn: John Cooter

10th edn: John Cooter and Joel Rickard

9th–7th edns: Maya Waterstone

6th–5th edns: James Burnett and Maya Waterstone

4th–1st edns: MPW

British Library Cataloguing in Publication Data
A catalogue record for this book is available from the British Library

ISBN 978 1 911067 74 0

All rights reserved. This book is sold subject to the condition that it shall not, by way of trade or otherwise, be lent, resold, hired out or otherwise circulated without the publisher's prior written consent in any form of binding or cover other than that in which it is published and without a similar condition including this condition being imposed on the subsequent purchaser. No part of this publication may be reproduced, stored in a retrieval system or transmitted in any form or by any means, electronic and mechanical, photocopying, recording or otherwise without prior permission of Crimson Publishing.

Printed and bound in Malta by Gutenberg Press Ltd

Contents

About the author

Jody-Helena Williams is an experienced psychology teacher having taught in grammar and non-selective schools across Lincolnshire and Nottinghamshire for over 10 years at GCSE and A level. As a former Head of Department in a Lincolnshire secondary school, Jody-Helena has given guidance to students on all areas of the university application process. Jody-Helena is a teacher at Mander Portman Woodward (MPW) Cambridge.

Acknowledgements

I am grateful for the help provided by Trotman Education and MPW, who allowed me the opportunity to edit this current edition. I am also grateful to those who worked on the earlier editions. Thank you also to the British Psychological Society, whose excellent website and range of publications made the job of writing this guide much easier, to the Higher Education Academy, to the academics who contributed quotes and to UCAS. Many thanks to the University of Liverpool for the kind permission to publish the course outline. Special thanks to Dr Philippa East for her interview and permission to publish her journey from a psychology undergraduate to Chartered Psychologist. Finally, I would like to thank former students who have provided quotes and sample personal statements for this edition, and to acknowledge the many students that I have guided through the UCAS application over the years. Much of the advice in this book is a product of what I have learned from these experiences and I hope that the reader will benefit.

Jody-Helena Williams
September 2017

About this book

Deciding what to study after A levels is a daunting task. There are already numerous books, guides and leaflets available to help you make your choice. So why bother to write yet another? *Getting into Psychology Courses* is, as the title suggests, specifically for people wanting to do psychology at degree level and so it tells you exactly what you need to know to get onto the course of your choice.

This book is divided into 12 chapters, which aim to cover three major areas when applying for a degree in psychology.

1. A clear and concise introduction to a subject that students might want to make a career out of.
2. Information on entry requirements, the length and content of the various courses on offer, and some indication of what it is like to study psychology.
3. Guidelines on making your UCAS application, getting work experience, writing your personal statement and preparing for an interview.

The 12 chapters discuss the following.

Chapter 1 – What psychology is really about – provides information on what the subject is really about and the different areas of psychology you will study as part of a degree course.

Chapter 2 – Careers in psychology – looks at the different careers a psychology degree might lead to, either as one of several types of professional psychologist, or in many other fields such as marketing, IT, teaching or social work.

Chapter 3 – Work experience – gives advice on work experience: how to choose it, how to arrange it and how to use it in your university application.

Chapter 4 – Degree programmes in psychology – presents an overview of the different types of psychology degree programme on offer and the expected course content.

Chapter 5 – The UCAS application – takes you through the UCAS application process, with particular emphasis on psychology.

Chapter 6 – The personal statement – gives general guidance on drafting a personal statement and specific advice for psychology.

Chapter 7 – Succeeding in your interview – supplies some advice on preparing for and attending interviews, where these are part of a university's selection process.

Chapter 8 – Non-standard applications – is for international students and mature students who may be making a 'non-standard' application.

Chapter 9 – Results day – looks at the options you might have on results day and explains what you will need to do depending on whether you are holding an offer or not and whether you have met the grades of any offer.

Chapter 10 – Fees and funding – explains the current fees and funding arrangements for UK universities.

Chapter 11 – Further information – gives contact details for useful organisations as well as a background reading list for psychology.

Chapter 12 – Glossary – If you are puzzled about any of the words used in the book, look here for an explanation.

This book is intended to complement, not replace, existing publications, many of which are included in the reading list at the end of the guide. If, after you have read the following chapters, your decisions have been eased in any way, its goal will have been achieved.

I hope that after reading the following chapters you will have developed a better understanding of what a psychology degree is all about, a thorough knowledge of the application process and a realistic appreciation of your options on graduating.

Introduction

Psychology is a very popular subject at university. According to UCAS data, there were 115,850 undergraduate applications to psychology courses in 2017. Only nursing and law received more applications than this. It continues to be a very popular degree course option because it offers a number of well-defined career paths within psychology, as well as being perceived by employers in general as a valuable qualification, as it combines scientific analysis, mathematical skills and the require-ment to be able to write coherent and structured essays.

Furthermore, many applicants have very clear ideas about which universities they wish to target. Some of the most popular universities have up to 20 applications for every place, although that needs to be seen in the context that each applicant for psychology can apply to five courses, and so applicants need to think carefully about the strategies they are going to adopt in order to maximise their chances. While there are a great many universities offering psychology, you are by no means guaranteed a place if you apply. This is why this book has been written: to give prospective psychology students advice about making a successful and convincing application.

Entry grades needed for a successful applicant

As with other degree subjects, the grades required for entry to degree courses in psychology vary from one university to another. Like most degree courses, psychology is very competitive, and many institutions can require top grades at A level. Typically, the older established universities may ask grades of A*AA to AAA, whereas some of the newer universities may have lower entry requirements based on points. Information and an online points calculator can be found on the UCAS website: www.ucas. com/ucas/undergraduate/getting-started/entry-requirements/ ucas-undergraduate-tariff-points.

Other attributes required could include having an inquisitive attitude, logi-cal and systematic thinking and a genuine enthusiasm for the subject.

> 'I chose to study psychology because it was something that was mysterious to me, until it became clear that psychology is a science based on rigorous academic research. As someone who is naturally curious and also analytic in my thinking, these two aspects of psychology made it an irresistible subject to learn about.'
>
> Josh

Given the statistical component of most degree courses, admissions tutors will also expect applicants to have a reasonable pass grade in GCSE Mathematics. However, you must ensure you check the GCSE mathematical requirement for your choice of universities as the expected grades can vary from an A to a C. You should also bear in mind the changes to GCSE grading from 2017; grade 4 is equivalent to a C, 5/6 is a B, and a 7 is an A.

> *'Applicants often need to demonstrate good numeracy and literacy skills, as well as the ability to handle scientific concepts.'*
> *British Psychological Society, 2018*

A previous qualification in psychology is not normally required for entry to a psychology degree course, but you may find that having GCSE, A level or equivalent in psychology gives you a head start when you begin your degree. The Russell Group booklet 'Informed Choices' (2016/17) says that a few universities now ask for an A level in either biology, chemistry, maths or physics to study psychology. This is supported by a survey by the Psychology Education Board of the British Psychological Society (BPS), which confirmed that 25% of accredited courses now require or prefer a science A level.

TIP!

Work experience is always helpful in supporting an application, as this demonstrates a genuine interest in psychology. Working in a school, nursing home or other care-centred environment will show the admissions tutor that you have really considered your degree choice. Work experience in business organisations can help too, for example in human resources, marketing or customer relations departments. See Chapter 3 for more details.

1 | What psychology is really about

Psychology is the scientific study of brain, mind and behaviour and is an incredibly popular, increasingly competitive course of study at university. Its popularity is fuelled in part by the growing demand for psychology graduates across a wide range of occupations, from health professions, to human resources, to marketing and communications, to IT. Students love studying psychology because it is eye opening, scientifically rigorous and readily applicable to life. Students are given the tools that allow them to see human relations and human behaviour through a special kind of lens, one that aims to give legitimate, evidence-based explanations for behaviour, rather than explanations based on common sense, proverbs or other metaphors. It is said that we are all 'naive psychologists', in that we all have our own explanations for various human behaviours. The trained psychologist, however, typically has three predominant qualities: a natural empathy, a strong background in scientific and statistical methods, and a drive to improve his/her own understanding that persists across a lifetime. The aim of this chapter is to give you an insight into some of the typical psychological research you are likely to study in the course of a degree programme.

More than meets the eye: explaining behaviour

Psychologists endeavour to explain behaviour, and no explanation is ever simple. Consider the case of obsessive compulsive disorder (OCD), a severe anxiety disorder characterised by fear, obsessions and compulsions. Although, from time to time it is healthy to be anxious in certain situations, e.g. going to the dentist or attending an important job interview, one in five people will at some point in time experience anxiety that becomes maladaptive, negatively affecting their daily lives and their ability to function adequately.

OCD has received much media attention in recent years, such as television programmes that aim to provide an insight into the life of OCD sufferers. Despite the informative nature of such programmes, they do little to address the root cause. OCD occurs in around 2% of the population whose daily lives are plagued by intrusive and persistent thoughts, occurring as obsessions and compulsions. With OCD presenting itself in a multitude of guises, going beyond repetitive counting, checking and cleaning, it is associated with embarrassment, most often referred to as 'the secret illness' and, as such, those affected often receive a late diagnosis.

Unlike some disorders, OCD does not discriminate – men, women and children are affected, regardless of age, gender and ethnicity, or socio-economic group. With this in mind, the explanations for its occurrence must be aplenty. We can all present numerous common-sense explanations; it is learnt behaviour from family members, influences from the media, or can we consider a genetic link?

Psychological theories consider all these theories carefully; however, some lack strong scientific evidence. Psychology is an evidence-based subject, and psychological theories therefore need to be supported by evidence-based research. This can explain why more historical forms of psychology, such as the psychodynamic approach developed by Sigmund Freud, are now regarded as unscientific and unfalsifiable. There is compelling evidence for a biological basis for OCD.

One explanation may be psychobiology: biological factors inherited from our parents. Evidence-based research would suggest that biological factors are implicated in the risk of OCD. Researchers have discovered that the COMT gene (Catechol-O-methyltransferase), which regulates the production of dopamine, is implicated in OCD. It has been found that OCD patients respond well to medications affecting neurotransmitters.

There is also a greater than random chance that at least one first-degree relative of an OCD suffere will have OCD themselves. For some years, clinicians have explored the role of heredity in the development of OCD in individuals. Paul's et al found that the morbid risk of OCD was significantly greater in first-degree relatives with OCD. A number of further studies have reported that monozygotic twins concordant for OCD symptoms. One study reported a concordance rate of 80% in monozygotic (MZ) twins compared to 50% in dizygotic (DZ) twins. Carey and Gottesman reported concordance rates in MZ and DZ twin pairs of 87% in MZ twins and 47% in DZ twins, giving a heritability estimate of 80%.

Despite this evidence-based research supporting a biological cause for OCD, some critics have questioned twin studies. Some researchers have pointed out that environmental factors have a significant impact on learning. Could it be that the high concordance rates in twin studies actually point to the possibility that, given twins share the same environment, OCD is learnt behaviour, rather than inherited? Further, it could be argued that Paul's evidence on the link with first-degree relatives is also questionable due to the shared environment and the possibility of learnt behaviour that cannot be ignored or ruled out. This suggests that we are not as much at the mercy of our biological make up as some research suggests.

So, do we look to biological, genetic causes or do we rely on learnt, environmental explanations? The 'nature–nurture' debate is one that comes up in many areas of psychology but more often than not the question is not so much, 'Is it nature or nurture?' but rather, 'What are the relative contributions of genes and environment, and how do they interact?'

With all the good research attempting to explain an important issue such as eating disorders, how are we to decide which, if any, is correct? One of the strengths of psychology is its capacity to draw on theoretical perspectives derived from different traditions, from biological and medical, to philosophical, to sociological. The psychologist understands that there are many things that impact on human behaviour and sees each of the various explanations as valuable contributions to a complex puzzle. This is why psychology degree courses always cover a number of perspectives and approaches (see 'What is psychology really like to study?' below).

Psychology experiments: revealing influences on our behaviour

Landmark social psychology experiments in the 1950s and 1960s banished forever the notion that evil acts could only be committed by evil people. Up until then, people committing outrageous crimes against other people were seen to possess some form of moral or character defect. While it is true that there are a number of dispositional (internal) factors linked to criminal behaviour, what these famous studies showed is that even an ordinary, everyday person could be manipulated into committing an evil act through social influences. Take Stanley Milgram's experiment conducted at Yale University in 1963, for example. By engineering a tightly controlled situation where participants felt compelled to obey the supervising researcher who was with them, Milgram was able to induce normal, temperate men into electro-shocking another man with volts that were labelled 'danger of death'. Only a select few refused the orders of the researcher and abandoned the experiment. Fortunately, in this case, the man who had supposedly 'died' was a confederate of the experiment who was only acting. The participant could not see him but, rather, heard his cries from the adjacent room and believed in the reality of the situation.

Milgram identified a number of powerful social factors such as uncertainty, agentic shift and graduated commitment that, if harnessed, could be used to manipulate people into behaving in ways that they would never normally behave. He finishes his summary of the experiment with a thought-provoking question. If he was able to influence a group of normal, healthy men to commit such acts of violence against their fellow men, how much more would a government, with its infinitely greater power and resources, be able to influence society? Milgram has given us a profound insight into the nature of atrocities such as the Holocaust.

Many other studies since then have confirmed the awesome power of social influences in directing our behaviour. One that stands out is Philip Zimbardo's prison study at Stanford University. A group of students were recruited to take part in a simulated prison. They were randomly assigned to take the role of either a prisoner or a guard and placed in an area of the university that had been modified to look like a prison. One of the most striking elements of this study was how quickly the people involved took to their respective roles. The simulation was supposed to last for two weeks but had to be abandoned after only six days, as people conformed so strongly to their roles. Prisoners became stressed, dejected and began to lose a sense of themselves, while several guards became more and more tyrannical in their behaviour. Even Zimbardo himself, who had taken the title of Prison Warden, began to lose himself in the role.

You may have wondered whether it was right for the participants in these studies to be tricked, upset and humiliated. Such experiments led to professional bodies such as the British Psychological Society (BPS) introducing ethical guidelines for researchers to ensure that participants are treated with respect, so that they are not deceived or harmed in any way and their anonymity is guaranteed. On the other hand, Milgram and Zimbardo found out things they could not have done otherwise. Understanding the need to weigh up ethical issues against practical considerations is now an important feature of all psychology courses.

Studying psychology will open the doors to a deeper understanding of human behaviour. When we are called upon to explain another person's evil act, many of us might say: 'He is just a bad person.' A student of psychology will pose the question: 'What else might be going on?' Such thoughts will then be developed into specific research questions and hypotheses that can be tested scientifically, for example in experiments, observational studies or surveys.

Taking a scientific approach: a way to explain human behaviour

Problems with sleep are on the increase. It seems that nowadays every other person has trouble dropping off to sleep or waking early. Similarly, every other person seems to have an explanation and a cure for sleep problems. How are we to determine which, if any, of the myriad explanations for sleep disturbance has validity? Do we have to go through them one by one, all the while suffering with poor sleep, until we find something that works?

Scientific methods, when applied to psychological issues, provide us with a powerful way of determining those explanations that are valid and those that should be confined to the realms of 'folk' psychology – interesting ideas that lack any true power.

The placebo effect, for example, is one anomaly that can point us in the right direction. This effect shows the power of belief to heal; a person given a sugar pill (medically ineffective) who believes it to be actual medication can recover more rapidly from illness. This shows us that any treatment for a psychological problem must demonstrate its effectiveness over a placebo, or else the treatment is no better than wishful thinking. We can do this by dividing a sample of people with the illness into two groups and treating half with the placebo and half with the actual treatment.

In light of this, we can surely separate out explanations for sleep problems into two categories: explanations that have been the subject of a controlled experiment, or explanations that have come about anecdotally from someone who has had a single experience and is passionate about the result. These single case studies can be compelling, but they tell us little about the true effectiveness of a particular explanation.

When it comes to explaining psychological difficulties that you or your friends and family face, do we rely on single cases that we have heard or read about for our explanations, or do we seek explanations that are backed up by good, solid scientific research demonstrating their validity as an explanation? What are the dangers of relying on single case studies, or the drawbacks of relying on lab studies or surveys? A student of psychology learns to combine different research methods, reflecting the complexity and variety of human behaviour.

Mind and brain: the rise of neuroscience

Philosophers and psychologists like to debate the difference between mind and brain. One way to think of it is to compare the brain to a computer: the mind is the software while the brain is the hardware. During the last century cognitive psychologists developed ways of studying mental processes through inference from careful observation of responses in lab-based tasks.

In the past few years fMRI (functional magnetic resonance imaging) scanners and PET (positron emission tomography) scans have increasingly been used to map the functions of the brain. Journalists like reporting on the latest advances in neuroscience because this seems more like the layperson's idea of science and the colourful brain-scan images look great in newspapers.

Cognitive neuropsychology uses these techniques to shed light on mental processes. Cognitive psychology is concerned with mental processes such as perception, attention, reasoning and memory. For example, 40 years ago medical case studies and lab experiments led to the proposal of models of working memory, as distinct from long-term memory. Placing someone in a scanner and giving them various memory tests can now permit us to see the areas of the brain involved in different aspects of working memory.

However, some psychologists have been critical of the excitement about neuroscience, pointing out that a good deal of research just locates the site of mental functions which we knew must be carried out somewhere in the brain anyway. Either way, neuropsychology is still in its infancy and it is likely that this technological approach will produce more and more insights into the functioning of mind and brain in the future. University courses are increasingly reflecting this in their content and there is more of an emphasis on biology.

We're all the same but we're all different: the study of individual differences

Are people becoming more or less aggressive? Why does anorexia occur only in some countries? What makes one person more intelligent than another? Why do some people form secure and lasting relationships, while others are married and divorced several times? Society is always asking these questions and psychologists attempt to answer them. For instance, we can devise tests to measure levels of aggression and then manipulate different factors such as the level of violence in a video game to see what effect it might have on people's aggressiveness. Or we could give people questionnaires about their family background and their attitudes to relationships that would enable us to look for links between early experiences and adult behaviour.

Taking the example of aggression again, an evolutionary psychologist would be interested in aggression as an inherited human instinct and the adaptive function that it played in the life of our early ancestors, while a social psychologist would ask how present-day social situations make people aggressive.

By contrast, the individual differences approach is interested in measuring the relative aggressiveness of individuals and attempting to identify the factors that account for the differences between them. This approach has been applied for much of the history of psychology to measure intelligence, personality or psychological abnormalities. Most of us will have taken some kind of psychological test at one time or other, maybe an IQ test, or a personality test that rates how much of an extrovert or introvert we are.

Psychometric tests are big business, with a number of organisations devoted to producing reliable and valid tests for use in all kinds of settings: in education, prisons, the armed services, the health service or businesses. These tests are all aimed at assessing people's suitability for something: training, a job or some form of treatment perhaps (known as an 'intervention').

However, some psychologists ask whether giving someone a score on a personality scale really tells us much about the uniqueness of that person as an individual. Such researchers might favour a qualitative approach, interviewing people to get an in-depth understanding of personal worlds. Others have denied that personality is stable or predictable at all, arguing that psychometric tests are too influenced by social desirability or the context in which they are completed. At university you will be able to explore such debates further and if you go on to a career in psychology you are likely to use or even design psychometric tests.

Making a real difference to people's lives: psychotherapy

Imagine yourself sitting in front of a psychotherapist for the first time. Having struggled for some time with constant self-criticism, depression and intense anxiety that seems to come from nowhere (always at the most inconvenient times), you have finally summoned the courage to ask for help. Fifty years ago, the therapist would most likely have been psychoanalytic, taking their lead from pioneers like Sigmund Freud. Your current struggles would be explained as the result of unresolved conflicts residing deep within your unconscious and it would be the therapist's job to help bring those issues to your awareness, perhaps through hypnosis, dream interpretation or free association, so that you could 'work them through'.

Modern psychological treatments, or 'talk-therapies', have developed over the last 30–40 years which focus on present, conscious thoughts, and have begun what is amounting to a revolution in the field of mental health. Aaron Beck, inventor of cognitive behaviour therapy (CBT), shows us that our immediate thought patterns cause us to interpret the world in systematic ways, sometimes ensnaring us in a tangle of negative or self-defeating thoughts. Such dysfunctional beliefs and thought processes are responsible for negative emotions and maladaptive behaviour. In comparison to traditional psychoanalytic approaches, which can take many years to unravel a person's neuroses, CBT is quick and targets our illogical or dysfunctional thoughts from day one.

Controlled studies have demonstrated that CBT is at least as effective as antidepressant drugs for mild to moderate depression. This is just one area of psychology that not only stands up to scientific scrutiny but also has a profoundly positive impact on the human race as a whole. The CBT approach is used in a number of areas of mental health and has also been adopted by coaching psychologists, who are engaged to improve performance and well-being in a range of contexts from sport to business.

While an undergraduate degree will not train you to be a psychotherapist, students who enter postgraduate training in clinical or counselling psychology will learn these skills.

What is psychology really like to study?

Psychology is an increasingly popular subject of study, with 150 higher education institutions offering degree-level courses in the subject either as free-standing degree programmes in their own right or as modules in other combined programmes. Despite this growth in student places, there are still, however, some popular misconceptions about the content of degree programmes. They do not offer students the chance to spend three years studying the works of Freud. Nor do they enable you to see into other people's innermost thoughts. In particular, a psychology degree does not qualify you to work as a therapist or counsellor.

Psychology is taught as a **scientific** subject and students spend most of their time studying the results of research into human behaviour and theories that are based on experimental findings.

What is it like to study psychology at university?

'Studying psychology is fun. We have a mixture of standard stats lectures, but also outstanding evidence and enquiry lectures where the format is completely different. We have to answer questions such as "Where is my mind?", "Can you sue a casino?", "Where do superstitions come from?", "Are we just robots?" and even "Why do cowboys fight?" Definitely not what I expected from lectures. The course at UCL (University College London) covers almost all areas in psychology, especially in the third year when it allows students to go deeper into areas that interest them. With two elective modules in year one, students can still retain their interest in other psychology-unrelated subjects such as business and management, mathematics or pharmacology. For example, I study Forensic Psychology and Children's Language Development as my electives. Independent study mainly involves lots of reading. It's usually up to 10 references for every lecture so trying to keep up with the volume of work can be difficult. We have lab sessions too involving lots of statistics, working with computers and acting as participants in our own research. Sometimes it involves deception and use of confederates (fake participants).'

Aizhan

'I haven't found any difficulty understanding the concepts on the course. At first I believed that my existing level of essay skill would be adequate, but I soon found out that the amount of independent research and creative thought is much greater than is expected at A level. I have enjoyed this challenge, which I know is raising my intellect to a higher academic level. In the first year everyone studies the same syllabus. There is quite a lot of overlap with A level Psychology and it is helpful to have done that but there are quite a lot of people who haven't. We have taken part in some interesting activities to learn research skills. One was an exercise on perception of attractiveness where we acted as participants, then analysed the data we had collected. We also examined self-esteem, first defining it in groups, then measuring the validity of a questionnaire and identifying overlapping traits. There is a "Challenge Week" in which we give presentations on a topic of our own choice. I would say about 75% of the course demands independent study, especially for essays, where we need to find our own references and work out our own critical evaluation. There is an exam each semester, 60% of which is based on multiple-choice questions. In the second year there are options depending whether we are considering a career in business or a more scientific future.'

Jinseo

'The thing I have enjoyed most is just having the chance to experience being a university student. I have found difficult the greater emphasis on independence, especially in terms of organising yourself and time management, along with APA [American Psychological Association] style referencing and citations which comply with academic journal standards. A levels prepare you well for writing essays. Also the emphasis on research methods in psychology and other science A levels prepares you for the university module on this topic. Background reading is very useful as it helps to familiarise you with different areas of psychology and this is great for your confidence.'

Josh

'I have enjoyed studying health psychology and clinical psychology, which is very interesting. I am not too sure yet about research methods and statistics! However, we get lots of help from the lecturers. A level Psychology has helped a lot but is not essential, in fact nearly a quarter of the students on the course did not take it. Many of the topics come up again.'

Electra

'I have particularly enjoyed learning about the more scientific modules, such as Cognitive Psychology and Neuropsychology, as I am very interested in the mind and its functions. As with *any degree, there have been modules which I have not enjoyed as much, such as statistics. The statistics module is a compulsory module for both first- and second-year students and, although I did not particularly enjoy the module, studying it has prepared me for using the statistical methods that are required for my third-year project. As well as this, there is always help at hand for any difficulties that students may experience with the modules that they are studying. In my first year of university I found the weekly workshops extremely helpful as I was able to discuss any misunderstandings regarding the content in lectures with the members of staff. I also found it useful that the lecturers have an open-door policy, which allows students to approach their lecturers at any time if they have any questions regarding the content covered in lectures.'*

Sweena

On a degree course you will learn about a great deal of published research and you will also carry out some yourself. Just as psychology embraces a range of theoretical perspectives, it also employs a variety of methodologies, so you are likely to gain experience of different approaches to research such as experiments, observational studies, surveys and interviews.

The examples in the sections above are just an indication of the many different topics you might study for a psychology degree. On a BPS-accredited course you will cover all of the following areas.

- **Biological psychology:** how the brain influences behaviour, the effects of hormones, how it can be affected by drugs.
- **Cognitive psychology:** how we remember, learn, think, reason, perceive, speak and understand.
- **Developmental psychology:** how humans develop physically, mentally and socially during childhood and adolescence and their lifespan.
- **Social psychology:** how human behaviour and experience are affected by social context such as in groups and relationships.
- **Conceptual and historical issues:** how psychological explanations have changed over time, and key debates that shape the future of psychology.
- **Individual differences:** consider the differences rather than the similarities between people, such as in personality.
- **Research methods:** quantitative and qualitative methods, research design, data collection, analysis and interpretation.

'There is no doubt that A level Psychology has made it easier to tackle studying the subject at degree level. I had come across many of the theories and research studies previously and I was familiar with much of the technical language as well as the methodologies. Of course, some topics are completely new to me, but past experience of studying psychology gave me a framework to analyse and understand them.'

Jinseo

Why is psychology so popular?

Overall, then, why is psychology such a popular subject for a first degree? There are several reasons.

Potential students are attracted to a subject that gives them insights into human behaviour, and students of psychology need to have a basic interest in other people and themselves.

'I was attracted to psychology because I wanted to understand myself more, as well as other people around me.'

Electra

'From having studied psychology at A level, I knew immediately that I wanted to study psychology at a further level. The scientific aspects particularly interested me and the fact that I would be able to study a subject that would allow me to apply my knowledge to help others greatly appealed to me.'

Sweena

It is a particularly attractive subject for mature students, who may already have touched on the subject during previous training. Business managers, nurses and social services staff may well have been introduced to some of the basic concepts in psychology and want to learn more.

Although now classed as a science, psychology is a subject that can be seen to span both arts and science subjects. It attracts students who have broadly based interests and abilities, who do not want to be seen as either an 'arts' or a 'science' person. A background in philosophy or languages can be as relevant as one in biology or mathematics. That said, those with some science background will be at an advantage due to the focus on scientific methods. Don't be put off if you have an arts background though, as enthusiasm for the subject, open-mindedness and willingness to learn new skills are just as important.

> *'During an art residential course I was particularly intrigued by different people's perception of beauty and also by the use of the "golden section". I was also interested in the fact that sometimes specific relationships are singled out for attention in a painting, for example in Edgar Degas's* The Bellihi *he is portraying the tension between family members.'*
>
> *Andrea*

Finally, although the subject of psychology has been studied at university level for a century – the first professor of psychology was appointed in 1919 – it is still seen as a comparatively 'new' subject and, because of the volume of research carried out around the world, students will be studying a subject in which the boundaries of knowledge are constantly changing. What is more, as a result of the diverse applications of psychology in, for example, healthcare, sports psychology and organisational development, many new and exciting work opportunities are being created.

2| Careers in psychology

It is important to consider the career you wish to follow after completing your degree, as this may affect the type of psychology course you choose to take. Depending on your own reasons for studying the subject, a psychology degree can be seen as either academic (such as English) or vocational (like medicine). The number of psychology graduates vastly outweighs the number of openings for professional psychologists. In fact the Higher Education Academy (HEA) estimated that only about 20% of psychology graduates go on to become Chartered Psychologists.

An accredited degree in psychology can be the first step towards becoming a psychologist, but it will also give you valuable skills that can be used in a variety of sectors. A report by a group of leading psychologists representing the BPS, the HEA and the Association of Heads of Psychology Departments concluded that an accredited UK undergraduate psychology programme has three main strengths.

1. It covers a wide range of approaches and methodologies, all focused on understanding human behaviour.
2. It provides for great flexibility in choice of future career, in psychology or elsewhere.
3. It develops self-critical ability, creating the motivation and capacity to develop and to meet change.

Psychology graduates are highly regarded by employers and have a good chance of finding employment. This is because the skills they acquire are transferable across many careers. The latest graduate research from the Higher Education Careers Services Unit (HECSU), *What do graduates do?* (2017), shows that six months after graduation 58.6% of psychology graduates were employed – higher than the rate for all other science degrees, with only economics and sociology graduates from the social sciences reporting higher employment rates. Meanwhile, 20.7% of psychology graduates were in further study, compared with 12.1% on average of graduates across all other subjects. The relatively high figure of psychology graduates continuing with their studies is an indication of the need to gain further qualifications in order to practise as a psychologist.

There are essentially three main career routes for those who complete a degree course in psychology.

1. To train as a professional psychologist by completing several years of further study and training at postgraduate level.
2. To enter work or postgraduate training that builds on or relates to knowledge gained during a psychology degree programme.
3. To find a graduate-level career which is unrelated to psychology but which may reflect your particular skills and interests.

> For more information about psychology as a career, you should look at the British Psychological Society's website: www.bps.org.uk

The three routes are outlined in more detail below to give you an idea of what you might expect after three or four years of study.

Professional psychology

Statutory regulation for psychologists in the UK was introduced in 2009. Nine specialist titles are now protected by law and regulated by the Health and Care Professions Council (HCPC), which has the responsibility for maintaining a register of practitioner psychologists. The regulated titles are:

- practitioner psychologist
- registered psychologist
- clinical psychologist
- counselling psychologist
- educational psychologist
- forensic psychologist
- health psychologist
- neuropsychologist
- occupational psychologist
- sport and exercise psychologist.

You cannot practise under one of these titles without taking the necessary training and becoming chartered via the BPS. As a rule of thumb, you will need a doctorate level qualification for any of these roles.

As an undergraduate on an accredited degree you can join the BPS as a student member and get the monthly members' magazine *The Psychologist*. This publishes employment ads for psychologists, which can give you a good idea of the type of work, the range of employers and the remuneration that can be expected.

Studying for a career in psychology takes on average seven years (including the three or four years for your undergraduate degree), but this can vary depending on your academic profile to date and the type of psychology you want to practise. If you wish to be a professional psychologist you must ensure that your degree will give you the Graduate Basis for Chartered Membership (GBC) of the BPS. This is normally gained by following a course that is accredited by the Society. Not all undergraduate and postgraduate courses are accredited by the BPS, and you will need accreditation if you wish to become a Chartered Psychologist. For a list of the BPS-accredited courses see the BPS website (www.bps.org.uk). However, if you have taken a course that is not accredited or you are changing career it is possible to take a conversion course that will enable you to move on to the postgraduate training.

Once they have gained accreditation, graduates will then have to start on a sometimes lengthy period of postgraduate study and practical experience to qualify for chartered status to enable them to practise professionally. There is often intense competition for places on post-graduate courses. For example, according to graduate job website Prospects only one in six applicants for clinical psychology courses is successful. At the time of writing there are 186 BPS-accredited post-graduate professional training courses in the UK. The main professional career routes are described below and illustrated in Figure 1 on page 21.

Clinical psychology

This is the largest specialism in professional psychology, and clinical psychologists work mainly in the National Health Service (NHS), Child and Adolescent Mental Health Services (CAMHS) and social services and in private practice. They work alongside other professionals and with clients of all ages to assess their needs, provide therapy and carry out research into the effects of different therapeutic methods. Their clients may be otherwise normal people who may have one of a range of problems such as drug dependency, emotional and interpersonal problems or particular learning difficulties. The clinical psychologist's role should not be confused with that of the psychiatrist.

Entry to training programmes is highly competitive and you will need a good class in your degree (a 2.i or above) as well as relevant work experience. This can be of two kinds – either work experience in some aspect of clinical care or community work, or experience as a psychology assistant working alongside existing clinical psychologists in a health authority. Vacancies for assistants occur quite frequently, but after working in this role there is no guarantee that you will gain entry to a professional training programme, which takes a further three years and leads to a doctoral degree. This final stage of professional training can take the form of either full-time study at a university coupled with practical experience or an in-service training programme with a health authority. Clinical psychologists require an accredited degree and chartered membership and an accredited doctorate in clinical psychology.

'After graduating I plan on completing a master's, specialising in clinical psychology, as I have thoroughly enjoyed learning about disorders, their causes and treatment. From a young age I have always wanted to work in a field where I am able to help others, and therefore I believe that a clinical psychologist role would be ideal. Working as a clinical psychologist involves evaluating patients' needs and abilities, and offering the treatment for problems such as addiction and anxiety. However, one of the benefits of studying psychology at degree level is that it is a flexible degree, meaning that the career opportunities after graduating are not restricted to just psychology-related careers. Many graduates have been offered a variety of non-psychology-related jobs – such as in journalism, HR and finance – demonstrating that the opportunities after graduation are endless. This is beneficial for those who are undecided as to which career path to follow as it allows them to experience several psychological fields but not be committed to entering a career in psychology. My advice for anyone who is contemplating studying psychology at university is to just go for it. The range of modules are guaranteed to appeal to everyone, regardless of what their interests are. As well as this, the content studied in the psychology modules is always interesting and engaging, to the extent where attending lectures does not feel like a burden.'

Sweena

Counselling psychology

A counselling psychologist combines psychological theory and research with therapeutic practice to help people to deal with psychological problems. Typically, these might include bereavement and loss, or relationship and family problems. The counselling psychologist usually works on a one-to-one basis with the client and tries to help them develop strategies to deal with life problems. Counselling psychologists work in a wide range of settings: hospitals and health centres, community mental health teams or child and adult mental health services, as well as in private practice, industry, education or business. To attain chartered status as a counselling psychologist, an accredited doctoral course or a BPS qualification in counselling psychology is required, following the GBC.

Educational psychology

Educational psychologists are experts in child and adolescent development. They work mainly for local education authorities, although you will find a need for educational psychologists in schools, colleges, nurseries and special units. The role of educational psychologists is to liaise with teachers and parents in identifying and assessing pupils and students with challenges such as learning difficulties, social and emotional problems, disability issues and complex developmental disorders. These can range from dyslexia, to depression, to disruptive classroom behaviour. Educational psychologists use observation, interviews and assessment tests to diagnose problems so they can offer consultation, advice and support to teachers, parents and the young people themselves. Their work and research can also be used to provide training to those working closely with children such as teachers, learning support assistants and teaching assistants. They also provide psychological expertise and training for teachers and others working with children. The referral of children with special educational needs to special schools is a typical example of a situation in which an educational psychologist's advice would be sought.

To qualify for this specialism requires a lengthy period of further study, training and experience. In England and Wales psychology graduates are required to have some experience of working with children or young people before starting a doctoral course in educational psychology. Examples of the kind of work experience required include teaching, social work, speech and language therapy or working as an assistant psychologist in an educational psychology service. The formal training is then followed by one year of supervised practice. In Scotland, educational psychologists require a master's degree followed by two years' practice for the BPS qualification in educational psychology.

Forensic psychology

Also known as criminal psychologists, people in this professional group work mainly in the prison service, although they might also work in secure hospitals, social services or in private consultancy with the police services. For the most part, a forensic psychologist's role is to modify offender behaviour, respond to the changing needs of staff and prisoners, along with reducing stress for staff and prisoners. A key part of their work is the assessment of prisoners in terms of their rehabilitation needs and their level of risk, based on psychometric test results and clinical interviews. In addition, forensic psychologists carry out research and put in place treatment programmes to change offending behaviour and often work with groups of offenders to achieve this aim. In addition, some carry out research to provide evidence for practice, undertake statistical analysis for offender profiling, give evidence in court to provide an expert view, and advise on parole boards. TV crime programmes and books have raised public awareness of offender profiling as an area that some forensic psychologists specialise in, but in reality only a few psychologists actually work in this area and its use remains controversial.

You would need a doctorate, or a master's degree plus two years' practice, for the BPS qualification in forensic psychology.

Health psychology

Working in a variety of settings – such as hospitals, community health, health research units and public health departments – health psychologists look at the links between healthcare and illness, using psychological knowledge to promote well-being and an understanding of physical illness. This can include helping people with behaviours that entail a health risk (such as smoking or drug use); preventative measures (exercise, diet, health checks); the delivery of healthcare; and the psychological aspects of illness, such as how patients cope with pain or terminal illness. They might advise doctors on the best ways to communicate with their patients and ensure that they follow the treatment prescribed for them. Health psychologists also work on promoting healthy lifestyles and may be called upon to deal with problems identified by NHS trusts. There are a number of accredited MSc courses for candidates who have achieved the GBC. Following this, candidates must gain two years' experience in a related field before being assessed by the BPS. A few universities offer a doctoral programme that is a full qualification.

Neuropsychology

Neuropsychologists work with people of all ages with neurological problems, which might include traumatic brain injury, stroke, toxic and metabolic disorders, tumours and neurodegenerative diseases. Neuropsychologists require not only general clinical skills and knowledge of the broad range of mental health problems, but also a substantial amount of specialist knowledge in the neurosciences. Although this is not a regulated title, a neuropsychologist needs first to be chartered as a clinical or educational psychologist before specialising and receiving further training.

Occupational psychology

Occupational psychologists are concerned with the behaviour of people at work. Their aim is to increase the effectiveness of the organisation and improve job satisfaction of employees. The specialty of occupational psychology is broader and less formalised than many areas of psychology and touches upon diverse fields such as personnel management and research. Occupational psychologists can be employed in a variety of roles for a range of employers. They may be employed directly by government departments, public service organisations or big corporations, or they may carry out projects under contract, either as employees of management consultancies engaged by organisations or as freelancers. Other areas of work include the Ministry of Defence, Her Majesty's Prison Service or as trade union representatives or a role in Human Resources. They may also work for companies that specialise

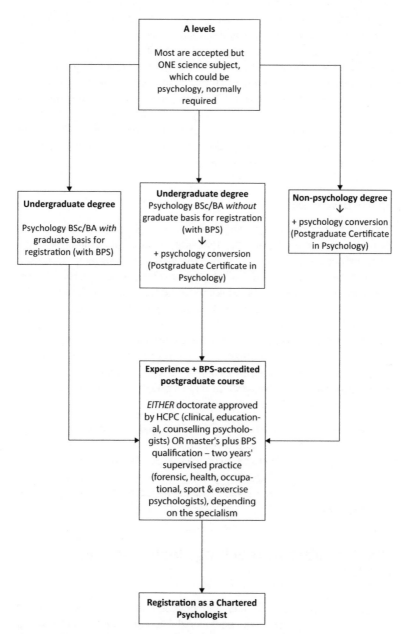

Figure 1: Routes to becoming a Chartered Psychologist

in creating and developing psychometric tests for use in recruitment and training. Within organisations, they may advise senior management on bringing in an organisational change programme, or they might be supporting the HR director in developing staff training or job design, running stress-management workshops or launching a staff attitudes survey. Occupational psychologists often advise on the tests and exercises that might be used for staff recruitment as well. They could find themselves working alongside IT professionals on the design of the interface between equipment and its potential users, or the development of computer systems. To qualify for chartered status in this field, psychology graduates need to complete a specialist master's course and the BPS Stage 2 training (doctorate level). In addition they must have three years' supervised work experience.

Sports psychology

Sports psychology is a growing field. Increasingly, professional sportsmen and women are using psychologists to help them to improve their performance. Many football clubs, for instance, now employ sports psychologists to work with their players on an individual and team basis. The aim of the sports psychologist is to enhance performance by improving the focus or the motivation of the participants, and to encourage a 'will to win'. They may also help referees to deal with the stressful aspects of their roles, advise coaches on techniques to build cohesion within a squad or among athletes, or support athletes dealing with the psychological consequences of injury. Sports psychologists can be involved in teaching or research or have a private consultancy caring for amateur or elite levels of competition.

To become a Chartered Sports Psychologist you need to have a master's degree plus Stage 2 (doctorate equivalent) of the BPS qualification in sport and exercise psychology. Should you wish to follow a career in sport psychology, you may find that coaching, fitness and exercise instruction and PE teaching will be advantageous experience and preparation.

Psychologists in teaching, lecturing and research

Academic staff in universities and colleges of higher education will combine teaching activities, such as delivering lectures and running seminars and tutorials, with a commitment to carrying out research. Their task is to keep up to date with the latest research findings in their particular area of expertise. They will spend a considerable amount of time making applications for research funding and, once the research is completed, writing journal articles to publish their findings. Entry to academic posts in psychology is very competitive. Lecturers in higher education are not required to have a teaching qualification but those applying for lecturing posts will be expected to have a PhD and to have some published research. Lecturing posts in psychology may also arise in colleges of further education.

About 3.6% of psychology graduates go on to train as school teachers, and according to data from *What do graduates do?* (2017), 6.2% of graduates enter the education profession. Psychology graduates who want to teach in secondary schools should note that psychology is offered at Key Stage 4 and 5 only (GCSE and A level). According to the British Psychological Society, the number of students taking psychology at A level has increased in recent years, creating a demand for qualified psychology teachers. For many years, a shortage of qualified psychology teachers has been problematic for schools and colleges but with universities now offering PGCE courses in psychology, getting into teaching is becoming increasingly accessible.

Other psychologist roles

There are a number of careers directly involving psychology that do not have titles regulated by the HCPC, several of which are in new and exciting fields for psychologists. People in these occupations may or may not have the title of psychologist but they would all expect to use psychological theories and methods in their work. Examples of a few of these are psychological wellbeing practitioner, assistant psychologist and clinical associate in applied psychology. Further examples are explained in detail below.

Animal psychology

A number of psychology first degrees now include options in animal behaviour, reflecting the growth of research in this area. Animal psychologists might work in agriculture, advising on the management and welfare of farm animals, or they might work as pet therapists alongside vets, advising people on their animals' problem behaviour and helping to retrain them. If you are hoping to work in animal training or welfare, it might be more important to study for a degree that specifically covers animal behaviour, or joint honours with zoology, even if the degree itself is not BPS accredited. There are also specialist postgraduate courses in animal behaviour therapy. According to the HEA there could be opportunities to work in zoos, laboratories, wildlife offices, eco-tourism, animal welfare charities or government departments such as the Department for Environment, Food and Rural Affairs (DEFRA), although many animal behaviourists are probably freelance.

Coaching psychology

Coaching has been defined by Myles Downey (author of *Effective Coaching*) as 'the art of facilitating the performance, learning and development of another'. Coaches use a range of psychological theories and approaches that are closely related to counselling but they work with people to help them tackle practical problems in their personal or professional lives and achieve their goals. Within organisations, coaches may be hired to work one-to-one with employees to help improve performance in a job, to provide stress-management training or to improve personal organisation skills. As with therapists, coaches may come from various backgrounds outside psychology, such as management; there is, therefore, no accredited route. Many coaches are self-employed.

Consumer and marketing psychology

Marketing as a business discipline owed much of its early development to psychology, being involved as it is with understanding consumer behaviour. There are good opportunities for psychology graduates in market research, which demands both quantitative and qualitative skills. Projects might include advising on product design, creating brands or studying customer lifestyles. Consumer and marketing psychologists might be employed by a big market research firm, or by a consultancy or work freelance. There is no postgraduate requirement but a joint degree, such as psychology and marketing or psychology and business, would be an advantage, plus relevant work experience.

Cyberpsychology

Otherwise known as human–computer interaction (HCI), this is an exciting and rapidly growing field that overlaps with computer science and organisational psychology. The possible roles are very varied. It can involve studying and advising on human interactions with all types of electronic technology, from games to smartphones, to aircraft consoles, to business software. Psychological techniques such as eye-tracking or behavioural analysis are used to understand the experience and satisfaction of users of technology ('user experience field') so as to help design user-friendly products. Another area is e-learning, where roles might involve developing online tools to support teaching programmes. HCI is also involved in mental health, from researching how to prevent or treat computer addiction to the use of video games and simulations to treat mental health problems. A postgraduate qualification would be an advantage here, especially as you could be in competition with graduates from related disciplines, but most important would be the ability to match your attributes and skills to the particular role.

Environmental psychology

Environmental psychologists are interested in the relationships between people and their surroundings. They study how we are affected cognitively and emotionally by the places where we live, work, shop and relax and how we behave in response to different types of environment. They are also involved in looking at the interaction between humans and natural resources and the related area of sustainability behaviour (e.g. recycling or reduction of fossil fuel use). A good master's degree would be a precursor to working in central or local government, or within a consultancy advising architects, planners and engineers.

Parapsychology

According to the Koestler Parapsychology Unit, parapsychology is the study of apparent new means of communication, or exchange of influence, between organisms and environment. Other definitions define parapsychology as the scientific study of psychic phenomena. Keen to show credibility in their field of research, parapsychologists' focus lies in collecting empirical data through laboratory and case studies. They study a variety of different phenomena including extrasensory perception (ESP), psychokinesis (PK), near death and out-of-body experiences, psychic healing and communication through mediums. Psychic research can be traced back to the nineteenth century, attracting scientists, scholars and philosophers. However, not all scientists accept parapsychology as a legitimate science but consider it a pseudoscience due to its failure to produce conclusive evidence. To work successfully in this field you must be open-minded and resilient due to the criticism of the field as cases of fraud have been uncovered in some famous studies. For those of you interested in pursuing a career in parapsychology, it is worth noting that it is a small and select field and a job is more likely to be found in universities conducting research or with a private research facility. Some individuals have made successful careers working alone, carrying out their own research and publishing their findings in books and on radio programmes.

Roles in psychology not involving a psychology degree

It is important to distinguish between the role of the psychologist and other professionals carrying out related work in mental health. As you will see, a psychology degree is not a precursor for these other roles but the training is at least as rigorous.

- **Psychiatrist.** A medically trained doctor who chooses to specialise in mental health by taking the membership examinations of the Royal College of Psychiatry. As a consequence of their medical training, psychiatrists can prescribe drug treatments. They will often work as part of a team with clinical psychologists.

- **Psychotherapist or counsellor.** Works with both individuals and groups to provide long-term therapy. They will often encourage clients to reflect on their past experience and early development. In theory, graduates of any subject can become a psychotherapist by taking a three- or four-year training programme of supervised clinical practice and seminars and, in addition, undergoing personal therapy ('supervision') themselves. For more information see the website of the British Association for Counselling and Psychotherapy: www. bacp.co.uk.

Case study

Alex chose to study psychology at degree level because he wanted a degree that would give him a choice of jobs after graduation. He did not study psychology at A level. Coming from an arts and humanities background (he studied history, politics and English literature at A level, and philosophy at AS), he was surprised at the scientific content of his degree course in the first year.

'I suppose that my research into the courses I applied for was sketchy, to say the least. Of course, I read the prospectuses and was able to talk about the courses at interview, but I didn't look into the detail too closely. In fact, it was not really a problem since I had good GCSE grades in the sciences and mathematics, and they gave us lots of help on the course. At school, my friends who studied mathematics always complained about statistics, and when I realised that I would have to do this as part of my degree course I was horrified! When we covered statistics on the course, though, it was relatively easy. It was similar with the biological content – learning biology at school was not very interesting because it all seemed unconnected with my other subjects, but making links between the functions of, say, the nervous system, and theories about how we think and learn made it much more relevant.'

Other psychology-related careers

There are several occupations for which a first degree in psychology is a useful entry qualification because of the particular knowledge or skills it provides. For example, an understanding of individual behaviour and social development is highly relevant to careers in teaching and social work. The study of statistical methods and the analysis and interpretation of statistical results can be useful in business and management, especially when devising questionnaires or examining the results of surveys. Any insights that psychology students gain into the nature of individual ability and aptitudes, and the ways these can be measured, will provide a foundation for a career in the assessment and selection of personnel. Knowledge you may acquire about physiological and cognitive psychology can be applied in ergonomics, or human factors design, as it is sometimes called. Yet again, an interest in other people's behaviour or personality may well provide the basis of careers that require an element of pastoral care or interpersonal helping, such as teaching, nursing, management or a religious calling.

As the *What do graduates do?* survey of 2017's psychology graduates indicates, around 14% entered legal, social and welfare work, 4.4% work as health professionals, 8.4% pursued work in business and finance professions, and 4% became education professionals. Other psychology graduates pursued options in marketing, sales and advertising, IT, engineering or arts, design, culture and sports.

> *'My initial idea, when choosing psychology as a degree subject, was to have a career as a psychologist (although to be honest I had not really researched this very thoroughly). We have lots of help with careers choices at the university, and I now think that I will use my degree as a "general" degree and try to find a job with a City bank. Although it might seem strange, psychology will be an excellent basis for this because of the need to constantly analyse information.'*
>
> *Steven*

Transferable skills

Many graduates in psychology will choose not to apply the specific knowledge of psychology they have gained from their degree course but, instead, will use the skills that they have gained in a wide range of other graduate-level careers. Indeed these skills are highly regarded by employers. Approximately 40% of all graduate job vacancies in the UK are open to graduates irrespective of their degree subject. With a degree in psychology, therefore, it is quite possible to train as an accountant or a solicitor, enter general management, become a journalist or work in information technology. Much will depend on your particular interests and the skills you have developed. In studying psychology, students are often surprised by the number of different skills they develop and which they can use in their work after graduating.

- **Information-seeking and research skills:** the ability to search databases and employ experimental methods.
- **Analytical skills:** the ability to think critically and weigh the evidence from different research findings.
- **Numeracy:** the ability to interpret statistical data and to assess the reliability of experimental results.

- **IT skills:** the ability to use software packages for data analysis and psychological measurement.

These are in addition to the skills that most higher education students will acquire, such as the written communication skills developed in essay and report writing, or the verbal communication skills used in group projects or seminar discussions and making presentations. As you can see, a psychology degree programme may help you to develop a broad range of skills that you can apply in the workplace, but you may need to make this apparent to potential employers.

Case study

Dr Philippa East is a clinical psychologist who runs her own independent practice in Sleaford, Lincolnshire. Philippa has been a Chartered Psychologist for 10 years.

'I originally studied psychology and philosophy as an undergraduate. At university, I was a student welfare rep and worked for the student Nightline. Over the summer after graduating, I did some volunteer work in the field of mental health, with odd jobs with local charities and services. I then was lucky enough to get a job as an assistant psychologist in an adult NHS Eating Disorder Service. In general, it's common for graduates to spend two to three years getting experience in the field of mental health (through volunteering, assistant jobs, research, or further study) before applying for clinical training. I then got a place to train as a clinical psychologist at the Institute of Psychiatry. Clinical psychology training is a three- year doctoral programme combining lectures, research and clinical placements.

'After graduating as a clinical psychologist, I took up a job in a community mental health team, and then in a specialist psychosis service in South London. I later worked for the Maudsley Eating Disorders Service, before relocating to Lincolnshire where I worked in the NHS Adult Psychology Service. In 2015, I decided to move from the NHS into the independent sector, and I now run my own therapy practice. Along the way, I've trained in a variety of therapies, including CBT, cognitive analytic therapy, and EMDR (Eye Movement Desensitisation and Reprocessing). As a clinical psychologist, I've also been involved in teaching, training and supervising colleagues, carrying out research, and consulting to services and teams.

'In a typical day (or week), my main role currently is as a therapist, seeing clients at the practice for their regular therapy sessions. I usually see between four and six clients a day (for an hour's session each). My clients have a range of difficulties, from OCD to depression, eating disorders to work stress. I also have time during the week for admin and liaison. This might mean responding to phone or email enquiries from clients who are thinking about starting therapy, or liaising with a current client's GP who might also be supporting them. On some weeks, I might have a supervision session with the counsellor I supervise, going through his own caseload and supporting him in his own therapy work.

'Once a month I also attend my own supervision, where I talk through my cases with my colleagues, particular any I am feeling stuck with. In between this, I might have some time to read up on latest research (e.g. in psychology magazines and journals) so that I am keeping abreast of developments in my field. However, the role of a clinical psychologist can be very varied, depending on the job and settings, and might also include conducting research, attend team meetings with other mental health staff such as social workers and psychiatrists, or delivering training and teaching.'

Case study

Qian Qian's parents wanted her to study economics at university so that she could work in business or finance once she returned to China, but she enjoyed AS Psychology so much that she persuaded them to let her follow a joint honours degree in Psychology and Management.

'My parents are OK about this because I will still get a degree that is business related, and I persuaded them that psychology will help me to stand out from other students and will also be very useful in running a business. I was lucky not only because they agreed to this, but also because my school allowed me to study AS Psychology. Chinese students I met socially, who went to other schools and colleges in the UK, were not given this choice.'

3 | Work experience

Psychology-related work experience is important to you both in terms of your university application and on a personal level. It has the potential to make your UCAS personal statement stand out from other applicants and it will give you something to talk about if you are called for an interview. It will also provide you with a better sense of what it would be like to work in fields related to psychology. This is valuable in itself and it will also enable you to make a more informed judgement about the kind of modules you would like to study during your degree and, in turn, about what career you might like to pursue.

Choosing the right kind of work experience

There is a good chance that you will have the same grade profile and a similarly good reference as many other applicants for the same course. This can make it hard for admissions tutors to discriminate between applicants. For this reason it is important not only to engage in work experience, but to consider how this work experience fits into your long-term plans. Getting the right kind of work experience will really help you to advertise your credentials to admissions tutors as a strong applicant.

> 'Unlike a lot of other people on my course, I did not study psychology at A level. I knew that I might be at a disadvantage with my application because I would find it harder to justify my choice to an interviewer. My teachers at my college advised me to try to get some related work experience in order to strengthen my application. I worked as a volunteer in a psychiatric ward in my local hospital once a week, and I also spent time in my holidays helping children with learning difficulties. Before my interviews I did as much research as I could on the related areas of psychology. It obviously worked because I received four offers!'
>
> Peter

As we saw in Chapter 2, there are numerous career paths in psychology. If you have an idea about what kind of field you would like to work in after your degree this can help you tremendously when deciding what kind of work experience you would like to engage in. For example, if you want to work as a forensic psychologist, then work experience within the prison service would be better than work experience within a hospital or psychiatric practice. Alternatively, if you want to work as a clinical or counselling psychologist, then work experience within a medical environment such as a hospital would be ideal. Below is a table to point you in the right direction.

Career area	Possible work experience opportunities
Health psychology	Hospitals, academic health research units, health authorities, university departments and also consultancy practices. You may get information about local health psychologists from your GP surgery or rehabilitation units in your local area. Universities offering the accredited Masters in Health Psychology will place their students on work experience, so talking to a tutor on one of these courses could also help.
Clinical psychology	Health and social care settings, including hospitals, health centres, community mental health teams, Child and Adolescent Mental Health Services (CAMHS) and social services. Most clinical psychologists are employed by the NHS, but some work in private practice. You might also want to contact the Clearing House for Postgraduate Courses in Clinical Psychology. It typically deals with postgraduates but its handbook gives information about what sort of work experience is desirable, so this may provide you with a lead.
Educational psychology	Local education authorities employ the majority of educational psychologists. They work in schools, colleges, nurseries and special units, primarily with teachers and parents. A growing number work as independent or private consultants. Try making contact with the Head of Learning Support at a local school or college and/or with educational psychologists, speech and language therapists, care workers or early years workers in your area.
Occupational psychology	Due to its nature, occupational psychologists work in many fields. The civil service is one of the largest single employers of occupational psychologists. The Prison Service, the Home Office, the Employment Department Group (including the Employment Service), the Ministry of Defence and the Civil Service Commission all employ occupational psychologists. Contacting them may put you in contact with leading occupational psychologists. Universities offering the accredited Masters in Occupational Psychology will place their students on work experience, so talking to a tutor on one of these courses could also help.
Counselling psychology	Hospitals (acute admissions, psychiatric intensive care, rehabilitation), health centres, Improving Access to Psychological Therapy Services, Community Mental Health Teams and CAMHS.
Neuropsychology	Work is mainly in regional neuroscience centres. Neuropsychologists also work in rehabilitation centres. Many senior neuropsychologists substantially supplement their income by undertaking private medico-legal consultancy as expert witnesses in personal injury cases, so direct contact with a neuropsychologist could lead to some form of work-shadowing with them in this capacity.

Forensic psychology	HM Prison Service should be your starting point. Forensic psychologists are also employed by rehabilitation units, secure hospitals, the social services and in university departments. Some practitioners also go into private consultancy, so direct contact with a forensic psychologist may lead to some form of work-shadowing with them in this capacity. Universities offering the accredited Masters in Forensic Psychology will place their students on work experience, so talking to a tutor on one of these courses could also help.
Sports and exercise psychology	Professional sports teams or national governing bodies of sport. You could also find work experience that involves sports coaching by locating the coaches of successful local teams or individuals. Many sports psychologists also work as private consultants, so looking through your local directory or online is a good place to start and could lead to some form of work-shadowing with them in this capacity. Universities offering the master's courses in this area will also place their students on work experience, so talking to a tutor on one of these courses could also help.

Making the most of your work experience

Before we move on to considering when and how to arrange work experience it is important for you to have a clear idea of how to conduct yourself when you are at your placement. Companies often take students on work experience so that they can have access to some free labour during the summer months. They get students to photocopy, file, shred paper and make the tea. There is a very good chance that these will be the kinds of tasks you will be given during your work experience. You should expect this to be the case and take on the tasks with a sense of eagerness.

It is also important to acknowledge that many jobs within psychology-related fields have issues related to patient confidentiality. This means that you won't necessarily get to see the kind of nitty-gritty that you might like to see. For these reasons it is very important that you are proactive during your work experience. There is nothing wrong with asking questions – and this is exactly what you should do. Ask them why they do the things they do in this order, or using that mechanism. Ask them why they have this policy rather than that policy.

Perhaps most importantly, try not to get left on your own during tea breaks and lunchtime. These are the times when employees will be able to have a more in-depth chat with you about their roles and what it is like to work in this field. It may even be a good idea to take a notepad and a pencil with you so that you can take notes. These notes will be particularly beneficial in the long run when you are preparing for possible interviews and trying to incorporate your work experience into your UCAS personal statement.

Work experience and your personal statement

If you manage to secure work experience that is relevant to your career goal it can really improve your personal statement. To understand this, consider the following two excerpts from these personal statements:

Example 1: 'My two weeks of work experience at Great Ormond Street Hospital for Children with the paediatric psychology service was a fantastic experience. It gave me a better understanding of how psychology can be applied in practice. It also helped me to improve my communication skills and my ability to work in a team.'

Example 2: 'My career aspiration is to work in the field of child psychology. For this reason I spent two weeks' work experience at Great Ormond Street Hospital for Children with the paediatric psychology service. During that period, I had the chance to meet doctors and nurses and listen to what their average day in a hospital is like, as well as find out general information on how they deal with patients to make them as comfortable as possible. I was particularly aware of the need to balance analytical skills and scientific knowledge with an understanding of the patients' emotional needs. This was a fantastic experience which gave me a better understanding of how psychology can be applied in practice. I am now particularly looking forward to studying modules such as child forensic psychology and clinical psychology at university. It also helped me to improve my communication skills and my ability to work in a team.'

The second example is superior to the first example in three respects. First, the opening line of the second example shows that you have considered how your work experience relates to your future goals. Second, there is more detail about what you actually learned. Third, there is a link to modules that you might study at university, which shows that you have researched the content of the courses you will be studying.

Demonstrating to the admissions tutor that you are thinking in this way can give you an edge over other applicants. The reason for this is that admissions tutors and their academic colleagues want to retain students throughout the entirety of the course. This is important to them because they want to work in a teaching environment where they feel that the students are genuinely interested and want to flourish. Furthermore, university departments are also under pressure to retain as many students as possible for funding reasons. When they decide which students they are going to give an offer to, they are hedging their bets on who they think will stay the course – so you want to show them that you are a safe bet!

When to arrange work experience

The simple answer is: as soon as possible. If you are in the process of finishing your GCSEs, then you are in a fantastic position to start looking around at the range of work experience opportunities that might be on offer so that you can select work experience that will be appropriate for you.

If you are in your first year of A levels you are also in a good position and still have time to get the kind of work experience that interests you. Ideally, you want to research your options and start applying before the Christmas holidays of your first year of A levels, with the aim of setting up some work experience for the summer months. There are several advantages to doing your work experience in this year.

- You can avoid the danger of simply trying to find *any* kind of work experience to put on your personal statement.
- It will be after your exams, so you won't be distracted from your studies during that all-important revision period.
- When you write your personal statement you will be able to state where you *did* your work experience and what you *learnt*. This looks much better than a personal statement where you state where you *plan* to be doing work experience and what you *hope* to learn. Again, think back to the admissions tutor who is wondering whether to take a bet on you.

However, if you are reading this and you are already in your final year of A level study, all is not lost – but you must get started on arranging some work experience as soon as possible!

What if you can't arrange any work experience before you apply?

If you are unable to get any work experience by the time you apply you can always say that you have applied for such-and-such and expect to do that later in the year. If you really can't get any work experience all is not lost: for many admissions tutors the most important things are your academic potential, your personal qualities and your enthusiasm for the subject. It would be sensible to check individual university websites on their requirements before applying though.

> 'Before applying to the University of Nottingham, I was nervous that my lack of work experience in this field would put me at a disadvantage compared to other students. However, the university is accepting of the fact that it can be quite difficult to get work experience in a psychology-related field.'
>
> *Sweena*

How to arrange work experience

One of the reasons why it is important to plan your work experience as soon as possible is because you may find that it takes some time to find the work experience you want at a company or institution that is willing to take you on.

Step 1: Getting the right contacts

A good way to start your research is to make a phone call to local companies, institutions and important associations, such as the BPS. Explain that you are an A level student looking for work experience related to a particular area of psychology and ask if they can help you. Sometimes you will get a 'Yes', sometimes you will get a 'No' and sometimes you will get a 'No, but I can put you in touch with someone who can help you.' The point is not to be deterred if your first two phone calls are a 'No'. Keep going! You could also send out a speculative email. If you wish to take this route, keep the content of the email fairly brief, make sure the subject is relevant and send out the email to one recipient at a time. Here is an example:

To: cambsedauthority@cambs.uk

Subject: Enquiry regarding work experience opportunities

To whom it may concern,

I am writing to enquire as to whether you have any work experience opportunities available. I am currently studying for my A levels in Sociology, Psychology and Mathematics at Cambridge College and am keen to pursue a career in Educational Psychology. Should you not be in a position to offer any work experience, the details of any contact you may have that may be able to help would be much appreciated.

I look forward to hearing from you.

Kind regards,

Catherine Harrison

Step 2: Sending a covering letter and CV

Once you have contacted people who will be able to offer you some work experience they may ask you to send in a covering letter with a CV. It is important to ensure that the content and the layout of these documents is clean and professional looking.

Covering letter

Here is an example of a successful covering letter:

18 Low Road
Cambridge
CB1 8ZZ

Mrs Kirby
The Educational Psychology Team
Cambridge City Council
Cambridge
CB3 2PY

1 November 2017

Ref: Enquiry about work experience opportunities

Dear Mrs Kirby,

I am currently in my first year of studying A levels in sociology, mathematics and psychology at Cambridge College. I am seeking work experience related to the field of educational psychology so that I can learn more about learing difficulties and challenges faced by students and the day-to-day activities of professionals working in this field. I am a quick learner and a reliable and enthusiastic worker. I am trustworthy and respectful of confidential information.

I would be interested in any work experience opportunities that are available. Alternatively, if you do not have any such opportunities at present I would really appreciate the opportunity to meet you at your convenience to discuss the nature of your profession.

Should you require references, please contact either my personal tutor and/or my employer. Full contact details can be found on my CV, which I enclose for your consideration.

I look forward to hearing from you.

Yours sincerely,

Catherine Harrison

Curriculum vitae (CV)

Standard CVs are a maximum of two sides of A4. However, unless you are a mature student, you will probably not have enough experience and training to cover two sides of A4 without leaving a lot of white space. For this reason it is better to have a full (but not cramped) CV that takes up just one side of A4. Remember that you are not applying for a job, so you do not need to overburden the person reading the CV with unnecessary detail. You just need to give them enough information to demonstrate that you will be a competent and hard-working member of staff.

In terms of style you should avoid unusual fonts and use of art. It is important to keep it clean and simple. The following are recommended.

- Font style: Times Roman, Arial or Calibri.
- Font size: 14pt for the main header, 12pt for the sub-headers, 11pt for the text. Just use bold for the header and sub-header; use italics or underlining for any lower-level headers.
- Font colour: black (and only black!).

In terms of content and layout there is no one correct way to compile a CV, but here is a suggested example of a successful one.

Catherine Harrison

Address: 18 Low Road, Cambridge, CB1 8ZZ
Telephone: 07896 435675
Email: charrison@email.com

Personal Attributes

- Mature and reliable
- Follows current issues in psychology
- IT competent in MS Office
- Empathetic listener
- Quick to learn
- Stamina to work long hours

Education

2017–18: Cambridge College
2018 – A levels to be taken: Sociology, Mathematics, Psychology
2017 – AS exams to be taken: Law

2011–16: Cambridge High School
2016 – GCSEs: English (A), Mathematics (A), Science (AAA), English Literature (B), History (B), Geography (B), Religious Studies (B), French (C)

Other Awards

[insert any other qualifications if you have them, e.g. grades with a musical instrument, Duke of Edinburgh's Award, martial arts belts, ballet exam passes, etc.]

Employment

2016–ongoing: After School Club Assistant, Little People Nursery
Responsibilities include collecting children from local school by foot in an organised and safe manner, organising a snack, setting up and supervising activities for children and assisting with homework.

The job requires patience, an awareness of risk assessments and Health and Safety.

[insert any other employment if relevant]

Interests

I am a keen hockey player and play for my local team. I spend my leisure time playing the piano and hill walking. I enjoy watching detective dramas.

Referees

Mrs Joy Bower	Miss Felicity Williams
Head of Psychology	Nursery Manager
Cambridge College	Little People Nursery
Cambridge	Cambridge
CB2 9PF	CB3 7UF
01223 123456	01223 789101
jbower@cc.co.uk	fwilliams@lpn.co.uk

Work experience interviews

Most of the advice and guidance provided in Chapter 7 of this book is applicable to work experience interviews. However, should you be called for an interview, here are some additional points to bear in mind.

- Conduct a little bit of research about the company or practice in question. Visit its website and read its mission statement and/or the 'About us' section.
- Remember to dress smartly for interview. It is always better to be overdressed and formal than underdressed and casual.
- Offer a firm but friendly handshake at the beginning and the end of the interview and be sure to make eye contact.

- Towards the end of the interview they may ask you if you have any questions. Try to think of at least three questions that you can ask when this happens, in case they answer one or two of your questions during the interview. A good way to show interest in the company is to try to find any (positive!) recent press releases or news items related to the company to ask them about.

4 | Degree programmes in psychology

When you are choosing a degree course in psychology there are several points to bear in mind. Firstly, degree programmes will vary in their emphasis. Some will offer a general but comprehensive grounding in the subject. Others will tend to specialise in one branch of psychology.

Secondly, admission to courses is usually open to students irrespective of the A level subjects or other qualifications they have studied. However, some courses, which lead to a Bachelor of Science (BSc) degree in psychology, may favour students with science subjects because of the scientific or experimental nature of the degree course and the ancillary or minor subjects you may be expected to take. Degree programmes leading to a Bachelor of Arts (BA) degree may look favourably on applicants with arts A level subjects. The distinction between the two is an important one, because the titles of the awards may reflect differences not only in main course content but also in the choice of subsidiary courses you can take. Those studying for science-based courses may have option choices in neuroscience or physiology, whereas those on arts-based programmes may have options in social or developmental psychology.

This chapter will look at the different degree courses available, so as to help you identify the type of course that is best for you.

What qualities should a psychology graduate have?

'The students we look for are intelligent, open-minded, somewhat numerate and aware that while studying psychology will provide them with strong critical thinking skills and knowledge of the complexities of the human mind and behaviour, it will not solve their personal problems.'

Dr B, senior university teacher and
Fellow of the British Psychological Society

'We are looking for applicants with intellectual curiosity and a natural affinity to science. This is often, but not exclusively, reflected in A level choices, and we favour applications from applicants who have studied biology, chemistry, mathematics, or physics, though having studied these subjects is not mandatory.'

Dr Marc, admissions tutor

BA or BSc?

At one time a psychology degree course might be either BSc or BA, but now the overwhelming majority are BSc only. About 70 undergraduate courses out of 500 accredited by the BPS offer a BA, or either BSc or BA, depending on final year options. A BSc in psychology emphasises the scientific side of the qualification being experiment- and laboratory-based, whereas a BA would often be studied alongside an arts subject such as criminology or sociology. In the past, a BSc tended to be advantageous in gaining employment over a BA. However, psychology lecturers at universities emphasise the importance of gaining a degree that is accredited. To ensure your degree is accredited, the 'find an accredited course' search tool on the British Psychological Society website filters accredited courses from non-accredited courses.

General or specialised?

Not all first degree programmes in psychology have the same aims. Some are intended to be general in nature, giving a broad and comprehensive overview of all aspects of psychology. Others, in contrast, will attempt to give a special emphasis to one aspect of the subject. You will see from the course details on university websites or in their prospectuses whether a course has a general or specific emphasis. Examples of specialised courses include applied psychology, experimental psychology, occupational psychology and social psychology. There can be some benefits in completing this kind of degree, particularly if you already know that this aspect of psychology interests you. It may also enable you to gain advanced recognition by the relevant professional group or division of the BPS on graduation.

Single subject, joint or modular?

Most university psychology departments will offer a single honours degree in the subject, which means that your principal subject is psychology but that you may have to study other minor subjects in addition, which carry less weight in terms of marks and assessment. In addition, there are numerous examples of joint honours degrees, in which you study psychology and one other subject to the same level. Examples include psychology and management, psychology and mathematics, psychology and sociology. This kind of programme enables you to study two subjects in depth, but you may need to check whether the overall workload is slightly higher than studying for a single honours degree.

By contrast, modular degrees offer a range of different subject mod-ules, often linked by a unifying theme. Often called 'combined degrees', they are typically provided by institutes and colleges of higher education and enable students to study psychology alongside other subjects in the social sciences or humanities. With joint degrees, and combined degrees in particular, it is important for applicants to check to see if the degree course is recognised by the BPS and gives the GBC. Without this, it will be difficult to qualify professionally. As mentioned, the BPS's website provides an online search for accredited degree courses.

Full time or sandwich?

Most degree courses in psychology are full time and last for three years, but some last four years, particularly those in Scotland, where it takes four years to gain an Honours degree. A small number of pro-grammes, called sandwich courses, give students the chance to spend their third year on practical placements in companies or with different psychological services or agencies. Students then return to their univer-sity for their final year of study.

Although sandwich courses last four years, they can provide students with a valuable opportunity to gain a year's worth of first-hand experi-ence, which helps them not only to develop new skills but also to make decisions about which career path to take when they graduate.

Students can take advantage of work placements overseas and in the UK. Before searching for a placement, you should think carefully about the type of job you would like after graduation to ensure the placement is worthwhile and complementary to your career advancement. Usually the university has a list of institutions and companies that it has an established relationship with. However, a lot of students secure place-ments through networking or by making speculative applications. Place-ment opportunities are advertised in a number of places. It is worth checking social media channels for opportunities or contacting compa-nies or organisations directly that interest or inspire you and submit a tailored application and CV. Most often, sandwich course students will make their own applications for placements but are supported through the process by a specialist team, who continue their support throughout the placement itself. The placement is assessed and forms part of the degree qualification.

A year abroad?

In one or two instances courses have a 'year abroad' option and arrange for UK students to spend a year studying at a university outside the UK, in Europe or North America for example. A year abroad will help develop skills and broaden experience as well as giving in-depth experience of another culture and educational system, building contacts and enhancing employability. Many of those who opt to study abroad say it is the best year of their lives. As for sandwich courses, universities provide support teams to help students select and apply for their year abroad options. Depending on where you want to go, it is not always necessary to speak another language.

Degree course content

It is important to realise that a psychology degree will have a big emphasis on statistics and research methods. This is essential for those who want to progress to professional psychology, but it also provides invaluable training for other careers. While A level Psychology can be helpful preparation for a degree course, experience of practical work and an appreciation of statistics gained from any previous qualifications (such as BTEC level 3 Applied Science) will be an advantage, as will be the ability to work independently. A 2013 report by the BPS concluded that increasing learner autonomy, statistics training, practical work and knowledge of contemporary issues in psychology will best prepare students to study psychology at university.

Most degree courses offer a broad-based introduction to the subject to allow for the fact that many students will not have studied psychology before. This will be followed by increasing specialisation and advanced study as the programme progresses. Undergraduate degree courses accredited by the British Psychological Society provide a basic curriculum in order to meet the requirements of the Society, so when comparing course and universities you should see some similarities in the structure and content. It is important to note that some course programmes may see a change in the coming years so always ensure you check the current edition of any prospectuses and the university website for any changes. Below is a generalised outline on how courses are structured across universities. For further reference, there is an overview of the course structure for the University of Liverpool's BSc Psychology programme for 2018 entry (see opposite).

First year

In the first year you will be offered introductory courses in different aspects of psychology as well as in research methods, statistics and the use of information technology. You will hear about some of the key debates in the field of psychological research. For example, how far is human behaviour learned or inherited?

Second year

Courses in the second year will build on and extend subjects studied in the first year. You may also have to complete a series of laboratory or experimental classes to give you a practical insight into psychological research methods. The results of your second-year assessment may well count towards your final degree result. Some universities offer a research project in the second year.

Third/final year

In the final year of a degree programme, students usually have the opportunity to choose modules or options that interest them, options that typically reflect the research interests of the staff in the psychology department concerned. At the same time, students will invariably undertake a major dissertation, based on a research project of their own choosing. This is a significant piece of work and the choice of topic may well have some direct relevance to a student's future career choice.

A typical course programme might consist of:

- **1st year:** methods and approaches to psychology; experimental psychology; statistical methods; social psychology; memory
- **2nd year:** research methods; further experimental psychology; behavioural psychology; cognitive psychology; developmental psychology
- **3rd year:** research project; option topics.

University of Liverpool - Psychology BSc (Hons)

Programme length: 3 years

The psychology degree programme at the University of Liverpool draws upon research excellence and a clear focus on transferable skills to suit a wide range of career choices. The degree is accredited by the British Psychological Society and provides Graduate Basis for Chartered Membership.

Year 1

Students take eight modules that provide an introduction to the principal topic areas and basic methods of research in psychology. Also in year one students have the opportunity to begin developing a specialist portfolio. Here are some of the psychology modules on offer: **Social and Abnormal Psychology, Cognitive and Biological Psychology, Development, Personality and Intelligence and Methods, Statistics and Computing**.

Year 2

In year two students undertake eight modules that revisit in depth the core topics of psychology (e.g. Social Psychology, Behavioural Neuroscience, Developmental, etc). The majority of modules are compulsory to ensure the students achieve the basic curriculum necessary for accreditation by the British Psychological Society. There are also two further modules, which are focused upon developing students' research skills to complete the training in psychological methods necessary for the third year research project. During year two students also have the opportunity to apply for 'internships' within some of the faculty's research laboratories.

Year 3

In year three students take eight modules in areas relating to psychology and assessments contribute to the remaining 70% of the overall degree classification. Central to the year is the 'Research Project'. This is a piece of empirical work designed as a platform for students to display the application of their prior learning to a research topic that can be related to their chosen specialisation. In addition, students are free to choose six optional modules from various 'pathways' to complete their chosen specialism portfolios.

First degree courses in Ireland

There are 28 degree-level courses at Irish universities accredited by the Psychological Society of Ireland (PSI). These include BA, BSc and Higher Diploma courses which the society recognises as conferring graduate recognition status in psychology. The pathways for further training to become a professional psychologist registered by the PSI are much the same as in the UK.

Katy, recent psychology graduate, Anglia Ruskin University

How broad is the course: what areas of psychology does it cover?

The course mainly covers social and developmental psychology with research skills.

How much choice was there in terms of unit options?

Choice was limited for our psychology modules, although we did get to choose which subsidiary modules we took. In the second year it is only psychology modules and there is no choice. However, we learn a wide range of topics and go into more depth than in our first year of study. The third year consisted of options plus the dissertation.

Is it mainly lecture-based or do you have a lot of independent study to do?

In the beginning, the course is lecture-heavy, but as the course progresses there is more of an emphasis on independent study. That said, despite many lectures, we were expected to carry out wider reading and research. However, our small class sizes meant that every lecture was more like a seminar with much student participation and lecture feedback.

How much practical work do you do?

The course was mainly academic and lecture-based although we did do practical lab work.

How are you assessed?

During the first year we were assessed by coursework and multiple-choice exams. In the second year, it is multiple-choice exams and essay exams. The only coursework we have to do is in statistics and practical labs.

Is there much overlap with A level Psychology?

I didn't take A level Psychology, I got on the course via a Level 3 Access course in Social Sciences. I found that much of the Year 1 degree content overlapped in terms of the topics, however this meant that I could focus on developing other skills such as critical thinking and research.

What are the hardest parts of the course?

For me, statistics, definitely!

What parts have you enjoyed?

I thoroughly enjoyed the applied psychology as this is where my personal interest lies. Clinical, lifespan development and atypical development were my favourite modules in terms of career progression.

Choosing a university: making a shortlist

With over 110 universities offering psychology and psychology-related courses how do you narrow down your choice to the maximum of five allowed on the UCAS application?

Things to consider:

- the grades that you are likely to achieve: there is no point in applying to universities whose standard offers are significantly higher than the grades that you are predicted, or eventually get
- the location of the university
- the facilities
- the course.

You might also find it helpful to look at the league tables compiled by the national newspapers. While all league tables should be used as a guide rather than as the definitive ranking of the university, they can be useful as a starting point if you are unsure how to start looking.

The Complete University Guide (CUG) (www.thecompleteuniversity guide.co.uk) league table allows you to look at the rankings of all UK universities, or you can narrow this down to just those offering your chosen subject. In its 2018 rankings of institutions offering psychology courses, the guide placed Oxford first, followed by Bath, Cambridge, then St Andrews. The ranking is based on a number of scores, including an entry score based on A level grades achieved by students joining the courses, student satisfaction, job prospects and research quality. The CUG website allows you to reorder the tables to reflect your own criteria, or to change the weighting of the individual categories. However, try not to be too fixated on the league tables; there are many excellent courses accredited by the BPS. Try to think about other aspects that you will expect in the place where you are going to spend the next three years of your life. You may find you get more out of the university experience eventually from going to one that is lower placed rather than one near the top of the list.

British Psychological Society accreditation

The BPS accredits certain psychology courses, meaning that graduates of these courses are eligible to apply for graduate membership of the BPS and for the GBC, which is required for the pursuit of professional training in psychology and is often referred to as the first step towards becoming a Chartered Psychologist. Note that eligibility to apply for the GBC is subject to achieving at least a second class Honours degree on a BPS-accredited course.

A BPS-accredited course will equip students with the following skills:

- effective communication, both written and oral
- analytical and evaluative understanding of complex data
- ability to retrieve and organise information from various sources
- knowledge of how to handle primary source material critically
- ability to work as part of a team
- ability to use scientific reasoning to solve problems and look at other possible strategies
- knowledge of how to make critical judgements and evaluations to consider different perspectives of a question
- ability to be sensitive to contextual and interpersonal factors, including social interaction and behaviour
- ability to work independently with thorough planning, gaining project management skills (see www.bps.org.uk).

If pursuing a career in professional psychology is important to you, you should consider BPS accreditation when drawing up your shortlist of courses. A list of BPS-accredited courses can be found on the BPS website (see www.bps.org.uk/public/become-psychologist/accredited-courses for details).

How to decide where to apply

Academic factors

There are many factors to consider when you choose the five courses that you are going to apply for. Some of these come down to your own personal preferences. Do you want to live at or near your home? Do you want to be in a campus university or in a large city? The only way you can really investigate these issues is by visiting universities, either by attending open days or by arranging private visits. But once you have identified the type of university you want to attend, you need to ensure that you have the suitable subjects, qualifications and predicted grades that will allow them to consider you. This requires research on your part, although if you are lucky your school careers department or university application advisers will have this information at their fingertips.

The best place to start looking at entrance requirements is the Course Search facility on the UCAS website, where you can search for courses using the UCAS Search tool. On the UCAS homepage scroll down to 'Courses' on the uppermost search bar and then type in 'psychology'; the website will then list all psychology courses. To narrow your search, there is a 'filter' facility in the top left hand corner which, for example, allows you to type in a city or postcode and will then display results in relation to the applied filters.

Once you have selected a course, you will be allowed to 'View' the university's entry profile and this in turn will give you the option of looking at the university's entry requirements. There are sections on course-specific requirements (what A level subjects and/or GCSE background they require, for example) and academic requirements (A level grades, International Baccalaureate (IB) scores, subjects that they will not accept).

Non-academic factors

You are going to spend three or four years in the university you choose for your degree, so you ought to think about some factors other than how good the psychology course is. For example:

- Where is the university? Is it in the north of England, Scotland, or the south? Is it in a town or outside? Is it a campus university or scattered around the town?
- What are the extra-curricular facilities? Do you want to be able to follow your favourite sporting activities, act or play music, or take up some new interests? Are there lots of clubs and societies?
- Is there a good system of pastoral support if you need help or for careers guidance?
- How much are the fees? What about the costs of accommodation and transport?
- And last but not least, what is the accommodation itself like?

How did you choose your university? Was it to do with the psychology department there, or other things about the place or both?

'It was to do with the place itself as much as the high reputation of the university. Having explored most of the cities in England and Wales I was attracted to Scotland by its history and culture, as well as by the people themselves. Despite more unpleasant weather than Cambridge, where I did my A levels, I was convinced that it would surely add to my life experience.'

Jinseo

'The fact that Nottingham is a prestigious university originally convinced me to apply. After attending the open day, I knew that this was the one for me. Not only was everyone friendly and helpful, but the members of staff and students seemed genuinely passionate about the psychology course. The department has been rated as one of the UK's leading schools for psychology and I personally have seen why it has been rated so highly. The lecturers and researchers are each experts in their field, while the choice of modules and the lecture content is interesting and current. I really appreciated the fact the range of third-year modules is so broad and there are a number of interesting modules to choose from.

There is something that can appeal to everyone, no matter what their interests are.'

Sweena

'The location of each university I applied for was of as much importance to me as was their standing in the league tables; this is because you know you will be spending three years there.'

Josh

'I was most influenced by the fact that my university was in the top rank for research excellence.'

Aizhan

'For me it was a combination of having a very good psychology department and achievable grade expectations.'

Electra

Finding out more

All universities provide details of their undergraduate courses online. Usually they will include a summary of the course, a breakdown of the course content and options year by year, the course requirements and a careers section. This may include information on career destinations of recent graduates.

When you have a shortlist of universities you might apply to it is worth visiting their psychology departments' websites and looking at the research interests of the academic staff too. This can usually be found under the 'Faculties and Departments' part of the main site rather than 'Courses'. Apart from getting an idea of what areas of the course different lecturers are specialised in, it might also give you a hint about what they might like to talk about, should you be invited to an interview!

You should also try to attend as many open days as possible. After all, you are going to spend three years or more at university, so you ought to make sure you will like the place. Open days should give you the chance to see the psychology department and meet some of the staff and current students as well as to see the general parts of the university (library, refectory, sports hall, bars, etc.) and possible accommodation. Visit www.opendays.com to find out details and dates for different universities and to book a place.

Sometimes students get the impression that universities are hidden behind a big wall called 'UCAS'. This is definitely not the case: the staff will be only too pleased to answer questions from potential undergraduates, so do phone them if you want to find out more, whether it is about course content or entrance requirements.

5 | The UCAS application

When you apply to UK universities, you do so using the UCAS system. The online UCAS application is accessed through the UCAS website (www.ucas.com). You register online at www.ucas.com/ucas/under-graduate/register, either through your school or college or as a private individual. Once you have received a username and password you will be ready to log in to start your application.

Planning your application

Before we look more closely at how to complete your UCAS application it is worth mapping out a timescale for completing your application. This is important because you will need to prepare for your application well in advance. A possible timescale might look like this.

Year 12

- **September–March:** Preliminary discussions with your teachers, family and friends – as many people as possible. Look ahead to planning open day visits and research possible work experience.
- **April–June:** Discuss your university options more seriously with your personal tutor and parents. You should also book open days and finalise work experience (see Chapter 3 on work experience).
- **June–July:** Make a shortlist of universities and courses.
- **August:** Work experience. Research courses in more detail, either on the university websites or by ordering prospectuses.

Year 13

- **September:** Complete your application and send it off to UCAS – it will be accepted from 6 September onwards.
- **15 October (18:00 hrs GMT):** Deadline for applying for places at Oxford or Cambridge.
- **November–December:** Oxford and Cambridge interviews.
- **15 January (18:00 hrs GMT):** Deadline for submitting your application to UCAS. If you do not get your application in on time your application will be forwarded to the universities but the admissions tutors will not be obliged to consider you.

- **February–April:** Interviews may be held.
- **March:** If you have been rejected by all of your choices, you can enter UCAS Extra. See the section further on in the chapter for more information.
- **April:** You will be given a deadline from UCAS to make your final decision around this time. See 'Key deadlines' and 'Replying to your offers' later in this chapter.
- **Summer:** Sit your exams and wait for the results.
- **Results day:** See Chapter 9.

The UCAS application

When you have logged in you will see that the online UCAS application has six sections.

1. **Personal details:** name, date of birth, address, contact details, how you will fund your studies.
2. **Course choices:** which universities you are applying to, and for which courses.
3. **Education:** past examination results, examinations you will be sitting in the future, where you have studied and where you are studying now.
4. **Employment:** if you have taken time away from studying to work or have had a part-time job this information is included here.
5. **The personal statement:** see Chapter 6.
6. **The reference:** this is where your tutor or someone else who knows you writes about you, your suitability for the course and, if you do not yet have your A level (or equivalent) results, your predicted grades. Each school or college will have its own guidelines for the staff who write references. Guidelines for referees can be found on the UCAS website, in the 'Advisers' section. Once your application is complete, it is then accessed by the person who will write your reference; he/she checks your application, adds the reference and grade predictions and sends them to UCAS. After that, you can keep track of the responses from the universities via UCAS Track (see the section on UCAS Track later in this chapter for more details).

Your referee will take care of your reference, and we will look at how to construct your personal statement in the next chapter. In this chapter we will deal with how to complete sections 1–4.

Note: If you are applying for universities in Ireland you will need to make individual applications for each university. Contact the universities for details. (See Chapter 4 for more information on courses in Ireland.)

Completing your UCAS application

Personal details

A lot of this is self-explanatory, but students often don't fill in all the boxes (e.g. where it asks you to state whether you have a disability, most skip selecting 'none' if they have none). Make sure you fill the section in as fully as possible.

One particular point that is very important is to enter the correct fee code. If you want to apply for either a student loan or grant then you need to choose '02'. If you or your parents/guardians are paying for university, then select '01'. Avoid selecting '99' (unknown). More details on fees and funding are available in Chapter 10.

Course choices

In Chapter 4 we discussed what factors you need to consider when applying for university courses. Entering the courses on your UCAS application is a straightforward process, but it is worth remembering the following points.

- Be very careful when you select the university codes and course codes. There could be a difference of one digit between a three-year BA and a four-year BSc with a year in industry – you don't want to get this wrong!
- You can apply to more than one course at the same university, with the exception of Oxford and Cambridge.
- The order in which you add the courses to your application is not related to your order of preference. The UCAS application system will simply order them alphabetically by institution.
- Remember to use your five choices wisely (or four for medicine, dentistry, veterinary medicine or veterinary science). Spread your choices across a range of entry Tariffs so as to maximise your chance of receiving offers.
- Don't forget to tick the box related to whether or not you are deferring your application.
- Don't forget to tick the box related to whether or not you will be living at home.

Education

This is the section where students are most likely to make an administrative error. Use the following as a checklist to avoid such errors.

- Do not enter any grades for any subjects that you are still studying at A level. You should input that the qualification will be completed in June and the result should be pending. This is important because entering that the result is pending generates a predicted grade drop-down menu on the referee's UCAS web page. Without this your referee cannot complete your application.

- If you have completed and passed an AS subject you need to enter this into your UCAS application. In this instance you should input when the qualification was completed (e.g. June of the previous academic year) and enter the result you obtained.
- You can enter the results of units if you wish, but you are not obligated to do so.
- Check that the titles of the subjects you are sitting are correct (for example, are you sitting mathematics or further mathematics?).
- Make sure you have entered all your GCSE (and/or equivalent) qualifications.
- Make sure that all dates that you sat your exams are correct.
- Make sure you have entered all the exam boards correctly. It is a good idea to gather up all your statements of results and/or certificates before you sit down to complete this task.
- Enter any other qualifications that you may have, such as Functional Skills or music qualifications; they carry UCAS points and some universities will accept them as part of your overall UCAS total.

Employment

If you have taken time away from studying to work or if you have had a part-time job this information is to be included here. You should include only paid work, not work experience. Sometimes students do not enter that they have, for example, been employed as a part-time shop assistant because they do not believe that it is relevant to their application. However, it shows the admissions tutor that you have a variety of qualities, such as the ability to work in a team and to be reliable. Moreover, the skills and qualities that you have demonstrated through being employed should be included in your personal statement. So, declaring your employment here corroborates any remarks made about your employment in your personal statement.

A final point about spelling and grammar

On a final note, it really is a UCAS sin to present an admissions tutor with an application that contains poor spelling and grammar. Often, via guidance from tutors, the personal statement can be relatively error free. However, such careful checking is then undone by the student spelling their name or their subjects in lower case, or misspelling their job title in the employment section, and so on. You must be thorough when you check for spelling and grammar not only in your personal statement but throughout your UCAS application.

Admissions tests

At the time of going to press, the Universities of Oxford and Cambridge are the only institutions requiring candidates to sit entrance exams. For all other universities, you must meet the requirements of their offer.

Cambridge

From 2017 entry onwards, the colleges at the University of Cambridge implemented common-format written assessments, to be taken by applicants for all subjects except mathematics and music. The assessment for psychological and behavioural sciences will take place pre-interview, in November; for more information, please see www.undergraduate.study.cam.ac.uk/applying/admissions-assessments. The Psychological and Behavioural Sciences Admissions Assessment consists of two sections: Section One consists of three sub-sections and candidates are required to answer two of these three sections. The Thinking Skills section is compulsory, and then applicants must select two from either mathematics, biology or reading comprehension. Each sub-section in Section One contains multiple-choice questions and 80 minutes is allowed to complete the entire section. Section Two consists of a choice of four written tasks of which candidates must complete one. The total time allowed for Section Two is 40 minutes. Candidates should be aware that calculators or dictionaries are not allowed to be used under the test conditions. The assessment test is designed to measure a candidate's suitability for the course and determine the potential to achieve on an academically demanding course.

Oxford

If you apply to study experimental psychology, psychology and linguistics or psychology and philosophy at the University of Oxford, then you may need to sit the Thinking Skills Assessment (TSA) Oxford. The test is taken at your school in the first week of November. You sit two papers, a multiple-choice thinking-skills test and an essay paper. The test takes two hours. Full details and sample papers relating to TSA Oxford can be found at: www.admissionstests.cambridgeassessment.org.uk/adt/tsaoxford.

Sample questions for the writing skills part of the TSA are available from the psychology course information page on the University of Oxford website once you have registered for the tests. You will be provided with a login and password. To give you a rough idea of the type of questions to expect, see the sample below. The question paper will contain a choice of three essay questions and you will be required to answer one.

> **TIP!**
>
> Please do ensure that you register your details in order to sit these tests. This can be done individually or through your school or college. The deadline is usually early to mid October and late registrations will not be accepted.

I've applied! What next?

Once your UCAS application has been sent you will need to register with UCAS Track, familiarise yourself with key deadlines, reply to your offers and ensure that you understand the purpose of UCAS Extra.

Registering for UCAS Track

Once your UCAS application has been sent you will be able to track the progress of your application on UCAS Track. This will require a new registration via the UCAS website. For more information on how to get started with UCAS Track visit: www.ucas.com/ucas/undergraduate/apply-and-track/track-your-ucas-application.

Key deadlines

The Oxford and Cambridge deadline is 15 October. If they are interested in your application you will typically receive an invitation for interview in November and the interviews will typically be held in December. Most students will then receive a decision after 15 January, along with everyone else.

If you have applied for all other universities by the 15 January deadline, then it is highly likely that you will receive a decision from all your choices by 31 March. If this is the case, then you have until a deadline in early May, a date stipulated by UCAS, to make your decision, which you do via UCAS Track. If you have not received a decision from all your choices by 31 March you will receive all decisions by the day after the early-May deadline. In this instance you will have until an early-June deadline, stipulated by UCAS, to make your decision. You will find a more detailed account of UCAS application deadlines at: www.ucas.com/apply/key-dates.

Important: check your emails!

It is very important that you check your emails regularly after your application has been sent, as this is the likely way that universities will contact you if they want to call you for an interview, invite you to an open day or make any further, more specific enquiries about your application. Some universities also have their own online application process that you will be required to complete and they will invite you to complete this process via email.

Replying to your offers

There are a variety of different kinds of response that you can receive from universities, but they all fall into one of three categories:

1. an unconditional offer, which means that you do not need to obtain any further qualifications
2. a conditional offer, which sets entry criteria related to the qualifications you are currently studying
3. a rejection.

When you have received the decisions from all of your course choices, then, provided that you are holding some offers, you must decide whether to accept or decline each offer. You can accept offers from only two courses. You can choose one as your 'firm' choice and another (normally with a lower grade offer) as your 'insurance' choice. You must decline any other offers that you have received.

UCAS Extra

If you have either been rejected from all five of your choices or you have decided to decline all your offers (or a mixture of both), then you can reapply for courses through UCAS Extra. UCAS Extra allows universities to offer places on courses beyond the initial deadline. You can apply only for courses that are eligible on UCAS Extra. A list of these courses can be found on the course search engine on the UCAS website. They are the courses with an 'x' next to their name. You can apply for only one course at a time through UCAS Extra. If you have either been rejected from all five of your choices or you have decided to decline all your offers (or a mixture of both) and you do not use UCAS Extra, then you will need to go through Clearing. For more information about Clearing see Chapter 9.

Taking a gap year

A gap year can be used to gain more relevant experience, to embark on personal projects such as doing voluntary work or simply to gain maturity or life experiences. See Chapter 3 for more information on work experience. Students who take a gap year typically do so either by applying for deferred entry or by applying after they have received their results.

Gap year route 1: applying for deferred entry

Deferred entry allows you to apply for university entry in the year after you complete your examinations. So, if you sit your final examinations in June 2018, you would normally apply for university courses starting in September or October of the same year. By applying for deferred entry, you apply for courses starting in September or October 2019, although you submit the application in the normal way using the deadlines set out above. To apply for deferred entry, you tick a box in the 'Choices' section next to the courses you are applying for on the online UCAS application. If you are going to apply for deferred entry, you need to give details of your plans in the personal statement (see Chapter 6). The advantages of deferring your entry are as follows.

- You can enjoy your gap year in the knowledge that you have a place at university waiting for you.
- You can embark on your gap year without having to wait until you can apply through UCAS in September – this is particularly useful if your gap-year plans involve travel or work overseas.
- You engage in more work experience or voluntary work. In Chapter 3 we discussed the importance of work experience. If you defer your university entrance for a year it will allow you more time to look for the right kind of work experience. This could be particularly important if you are not sure what kind of career you wish to pursue after your degree, as you could participate in several work-experience ventures across different industries.
- You can use the time to earn money for university, especially in light of the increasing costs in tuition fees.

Note: If you are thinking of applying for particularly competitive courses you must check with the relevant institutions whether applying for deferred entry will in any way jeopardise your application.

Gap year route 2: applying after you receive your results

Not all students who take a gap year apply for deferred entry. Some students do not submit an application (or do apply, but are not made any offers and so need to reapply) until they have completed their A levels or equivalent and have their results; that is, at the start of the gap year. Although this is not ideal there are advantages to applying after you receive your results.

- You will have your grades and so you can apply for courses for which you have already achieved the entrance requirements.
- You have more time to think about what you want to study, and where.

What happens next?

If you have applied for deferred entry your offer will be confirmed in the same way as everyone else's on results day. If you are applying after you receive your results you should aim to complete your UCAS application as soon as possible. Be sure to amend your personal statement to account for why you are taking a gap year and try to give as much detail as possible as to what you will be doing in your gap year and what you hope to gain from the experience. Importantly, try to convey to the admissions tutors the skills and qualities that you will gain during this time that will make you a better student. As you will already have your A level results there is a reasonable chance that you will hear from the universities before Christmas. Provided that (a) you choose courses that have entry requirements that you have met, (b) the courses accept post-Year 13 students and (c) you make convincing amendments to your personal statement, you will probably receive unconditional offers.

6 | The personal statement

The personal statement section of the UCAS application is the only chance you get to convince admissions tutors that they should allocate one of their precious places to you, or call you for an interview. It is therefore important to take great care in writing the personal statement so that you can convince them that:

- you are serious about studying psychology
- you have researched the course and your career options
- you will be able to contribute to the department and the university.

How to structure the personal statement

There are many ways of constructing a personal statement and there are no rules as such, but there are recommendations that can be made. Remember that universities are academic institutions and thus you must present yourself as a strong academic bet. You have a maximum of only 4,000 characters, including spaces, to convince the admissions tutor that you are well suited to a place on their course. For this reason your personal statement will need to go through several drafts, with your tutor, family and friends all playing an active role in helping you to structure it.

Getting started on your personal statement can be the hardest thing to do. Do not approach this task worried about getting it perfect the first time. It is perfectly acceptable for your first draft to be a long list of things that you want to say, in no particular order! You can then use this list to start to shape your personal statement into a coherent order. When you are doing this you may want to follow the layout described here.

Paragraph 1: How did your interest in psychology start and then develop?

The first thing that the admissions tutor wants to know is the strength of your commitment to study. Say clearly why you wish to study for your chosen degree, especially if you haven't studied psychology before. Wanting to work with people, or liking children, is not good enough. Give details of particular areas of study that interest you and say what you hope to get out of pursuing them at university level. A good way to achieve this is to start your personal statement by saying what first ignited your interest in the subject. This might have been a book or article you read, a TV programme, or through contact with a family friend who worked in the field. It might have been because you chose psychology as an AS exam. Again, there is no 'right' reason, but the admissions tutors will be interested in what started you on the path to your application. This would also be a good place to include any voluntary work or work experience related to psychology that you have undertaken or are going to undertake. For example:

'My career aspiration is to work in educational psychology. The cognition and development module in A level Psychology really sparked my interest and so I decided to take an after school job in an After School Club run by a local nursery. Not only did I gain hands on experience working with children of primary school age, I became aware of some learning difficulties and additional needs faced by children in education, which was a valuable insight. I met a Special Educational Needs Coordinator and was able to talk to her about her job and learn about some of the current issues in education that affect the learning and development of children. This experience has given me a real thirst for knowledge in the field of educational psychology and I cannot wait to study the modules at university.'

This makes for a nice start as it puts the 'personal' into your personal statement. You must try to avoid clichés that could appear in any personal statement. For example, it would *not* be very interesting to say 'I want to study psychology at university because I am passionate about the subject.' Well, obviously ...

Paragraph 2: What psychology research or study have you done outside of your A levels?

This is your chance to show that this application is not just a whim on your part, but the result of serious research. Many students think that psychology is only about the interpretation of dreams or why someone is attracted to someone else, rather than a serious and rigorous academic subject. You have to differentiate yourself from them by showing the admissions tutors that you have thought carefully about what a psychology course and/or career involves. Bookshops have sections on 'popular psychology' that contain books about psychology for non-psychologists – this is a good starting point if you wish to demonstrate an interest in the subject but haven't studied it at AS or A level. A word of warning: don't try to impress the admissions tutors by claiming that you have read degree-level psychology books, as you may be asked about your reading if you are called for interview – stick to things that you can understand and discuss. A selection of titles is listed at the end of this book in the section on psychology texts to get you started. If you have particularly enjoyed certain parts of your AS or A level Psychology course, say so and explain why. If you are new to the subject, give examples from newspapers, television, events or controversies that have appealed to the psychologist in you.

In this paragraph you could also make a brief reference to your other subjects in terms of how they relate to psychology. For example, 'History has helped me to understand the importance of considering the source of information and to analyse factors that can affect the interpretation of events.' It is also worth noting that some universities have been critical of the inclusion of Freud in A level specifications, so you need to be cautious if you decide to refer to Freud in your personal statement.

> 'What do I look for in a UCAS personal statement? First and foremost, a sound understanding of the subject of psychology. Students must demonstrate in their personal statements that they know what psychology is. Sounds simple, but should a student discuss counselling for example, this will ring alarm bells and I will call them in for an interview to find out if they are right for the course. A real winner is to demonstrate a sound knowledge of research methods and show that psychology is a scientific discipline.'
>
> Admissions tutor

Paragraph 3: What are your personal interests and achievements?

At least 60% of your personal statement should deal with material directly related to your chosen course. However, it is a good idea to dedicate a paragraph to extra-curricular activities. This could include reference to paid work, voluntary work (not specific to psychology), travel, Duke of Edinburgh's Award, sport and music achievements, and so on. Whatever you decide to include, make sure you advertise the skills and qualities that these personal interests and achievements demonstrate.

The following example is weak:

> 'Outside of my studies I am head waitress at my local Chinese restaurant where I have worked at weekends for the last two years and I have also completed voluntary work at the local Food Bank. I thoroughly enjoyed both of these roles as it has allowed me to work as part of a team.'

However, a stronger version might read like this:

> 'Outside of my studies I am head waitress at my local Chinese restaurant, where I have worked at weekends for the last two years. I enjoy interacting with the public and take pride in the responsibilities that being head waitress brings. I have also completed voluntary work at the local Food Bank, where I have sorted and categorised the wide variety of donations given (these include food, toys and books). The organiser of the Food Bank has been so delighted with my contribution and the manner in which I carry out my work that he has given me an open invitation to return at any time to assist with running the Food Bank. Both of these positions suited me as I enjoy working with older adults and members of the public. These positions demonstrate that I can be trusted with responsibility and that I am not afraid of hard work.'

Don't expect to be able to fit everything about yourself into the limited space available, and only include things that are relevant to your course or that you are prepared to expand on at interview. The idea is to whet the admissions tutors' appetite and to make them want to meet you.

Paragraph 4: Wrap it up and say what you will contribute to the department and the university

You could finish with a short, punchy paragraph that summarises your position and indicates to the admissions tutor that you are going to fit well into the department and add to the life of the university. Here is an example:

> 'In summary, I love the way in which psychologists take a rigorous, scientific approach to understanding people, the mind and behaviour. To me, it offers the opportunity to see the world in a different way and can lead to a range of career paths, including my goal of working as a clinical psychologist in a hospital. For these reasons I can't wait to study psychology at a higher level. Furthermore, I believe that my wider readings, work experience and extra-curricular activities demonstrate that I will make a positive contribution to any undergraduate programme.'

A note about deferred entry

If you are deferring your university application or applying for university after you received your results you will need to explain what you will be doing with your gap year. Try to be precise and informative. For example, don't just say that you are going to find some work to fund your studies. Instead say exactly what kind of work you are going to be doing and how it will help you prepare for university. If you cannot really say much about how it will prepare you for university, then you really should research work experience or voluntary work that will enable you to do this. Saying that you are going to work 50 hours a week in a bar does not come across as good use of a year out. Even if you need to work this much to save towards your tuition fees, you should still plan to have a few weeks off during your gap year to engage in activities that will prepare you for a psychology degree.

Sample personal statements

Example 1

I have always been fascinated with the driving forces in the universe, the building blocks of our being. How atoms form all we know, how every physical interaction involves forces of physics, and above all, how every single choice in our life involves psychology: the smallest choices, such as what we wear when we go out, to things like why we enjoy, like and prefer the rule of three. I have a burning desire to further understand the human mind and the untold power that lies within.

When I was in high school, I tried to help a friend through a spell of chronic depression without knowing how to properly aid her at all. I never would have imagined she had become suicidal. It was here I realised the human mind is every bit as delicate as it is powerful. It was also here where my passion awakened, and I vowed to devote my life to making sure nobody has to face what she went through alone.

I wish to major in Behavioural Science because I believe that by finding the root of a problem I can help more people than by sitting down with one individual at a time. Psychology is a legitimate field of science and can be approached as seriously as physics or chemistry, in a systematic and controlled way. For my A levels, aside from psychology I am also studying mathematics, chemistry and biology, further strengthening my knowledge to prepare for what is to come. I wish to approach the problems that plague the mind in a scientific manner, to find a proper solution to them.

Studying psychology as an academic subject has strengthened my interest and passion for it. The majority of the reading and research I've done has concentrated on the experimental and applied usage of psychology, such as the Stanford Prison Experiment, which opened my eyes to the fact that psychology is not a mere concept but a legitimate scientific field, as solid and observable as biology and chemistry. You can imagine my joy when this experiment appeared in the A level Psychology textbook. I was absolutely entranced by how the study not only demonstrated a total melt-down of character and behaviour, but also how it was able to approach and explain it in a scientific way, even when the problem presented seemed to be such an abstract concept. It also gave me the idea that nobody is truly born evil, and that the most ordinary people could become cruel and evil depending on the situation.

I am also interested in certain studies and psychological experi-ments that didn't go exactly as planned, such as the unfortunate case of David Reimer, the 'Little Albert' experiment, Johnson's Monster Study and even the CIS project MK Ultra. Despite the truly horrendous aftermath of these experiments, it is also undeni-able they provided essential data and results that furthered con-cepts of psychology, such as classical conditioning and the nature versus nurture debate. Not only am I interested by the findings of these experiments, but also the debates that have arisen in their wake. Do their significant findings outweigh the cost at which they came?

I was first exposed to the deeper concepts of the human mind through the Stanley Kubrick film *A Clockwork Orange*, where I was fascinated by the psychological aspects of the film: pseudo aver-sion therapy presented in the film and the underlying message that Alex represented man in his purest form. The implications and symbolism that it carried were amazing to me, and although I prob-ably didn't grasp the weight of them when I was younger, it has stayed with me and fermented in my mind till this day.

I once interned under a psychiatrist, and although I learned from him, I realised that it was not what I wanted to do with my life. I did not want to solve problems of the mind one person at a time. I wanted to identify these problems, and to push our understanding of the human mind and help contribute to all humankind, and I feel that the way to do this is through Behavioural Science.

Example 2

The scientific complexity behind how people think, behave and interact is what first attracted me to studying A level Psychology. Aspects of the human psyche such as our emotions and mental characteristics have fascinated me and have inspired me to pursue psychology to degree level.

A particular aspect that I found intriguing came about in the biological approach when learning the psychological and neurobiological influences on mental disorders, emphasising how a single gene mutation can stimulate disorders such as Klinefelters syndrome, completely changing an individual's life. I am keen to study this further at university level.

The study of A level Chemistry has improved my analytical and evaluation skills, allowing me to interpret results with great accuracy and draw up scientific conclusions, both of which are important aspects when carrying out practicals.

Studying A level Business Studies has also benefited me by enhancing my problem-solving skills and allowing me to draw up the strengths and weaknesses of a certain decision. Particular topics that I studied in business studies, such as data collection methods for market research, were reinforced in psychology enabling me to build upon my knowledge of methodology.

As well as studying A level Psychology, I broadened my initial knowledge of the subject by reading *Making Sense of People* where the neuroscientist Samuel Barondes gave an interesting grounding to how we all judge others in our lives and also how to assess and evaluate one's personality and character. Furthermore, reading *Thinking, Fast and Slow* by Daniel Kahneman provided me with his insight into remembering, processing and perception. Throughout the book, I was particularly intrigued by his insight into the two systems the mind adopts.

Having a strong interest in child psychology, I undertook a work experience placement at a children's day nursery, where I observed and interacted with the children as well as monitoring how well they accepted a stranger into their environment. Along with this, carrying out a placement at an elderly people's home involved me assisting those with mental difficulties. Here I was able to gain a greater understanding of the reasons for the vulnerability of the elderly. I considered this to be a valuable experience as it enabled me to appreciate helping others, a vital aspect in the psychology field. Finally, I undertook a placement at a radiography department, observing treatment sessions with patients as well as setting up MRI scans. This allowed me to experience a professional working environment along with reinforcing the importance of patient confidentiality.

Being part of the school Charity Committee permitted me to improve my organisation skills, think creatively and work towards deadlines as it involved organising cake sales, sponsored silences and fashion shows for charities such as Cancer Research UK and Children in Need. My part-time employment as a sales assistant at my local Mothercare store has allowed my communication and time-management skills to mature, as I have learnt to balance my academic work and recreational time.

Outside of my academic environment, I participate in playing rounders and have been the team bowler for three consecutive years. Along with this, I attend the local gym and have recently started the weekly aerobics and zumba classes, both of which are testing my physical abilities. Completing the Duke of Edinburgh Bronze award (and currently working towards the Silver award) has been a challenging, yet fulfilling experience, allowing my team-work and leadership skills to improve in addition to being able to plan under pressure.

Being extremely hard-working and dedicated to achieve my long-term goals, I am committed to explore the nature of psychology and engage with the critical and analytical work. I have a strong desire to study psychology in greater depth and look forward to the academic and social challenges at university.

Applying for different courses

You write one personal statement which is read by admissions staff at the five courses for which you are applying. Each university sees only its name and course code on the application that UCAS sends to it; your other choices are not shown. If, for example, you are applying to read psychology at one university, English at another, history at a third and so on, then you cannot possibly write a personal statement that will satisfy the criteria for each of the courses. Of course, if you are applying for courses with an overlap, such as psychology and neuroscience, you can write about the areas where this overlap occurs between the disciplines, but this needs to be executed with care otherwise the admissions tutor will be puzzled as to what exactly you want to study.

General tips

- Do not attempt to copy passages from other sources. UCAS checks personal statements with anti-plagiarism software: if you have used material from someone else you will be caught out and your application will be cancelled.
- Don't be tempted to get someone else to write your personal statement. It has to sound like you, which is why it is called a *personal* statement.
- Although you can apply for up to five institutions or courses, you write only one personal statement, and so it needs to be relevant to all of the courses you are applying for. You will not be able to write a convincing statement if you are applying to a variety of different courses.
- Save a copy of your personal statement so that you can remind yourself of all the wonderful things you said, should you be called for interview!
- If you are planning to do so, state your reasons for applying for deferred entry and outline what you intend to do during your gap year. For example, you might be planning to find some relevant work experience in a hospital, and then spend some time overseas to brush up your language skills.

Most important of all, prior to submitting your personal statement, read through it carefully, checking for spelling and grammatical errors or parts that could be changed to make for better reading. Do ensure that you save the document. This sounds obvious but the number of students who make a fabulous start only to have to begin again because they didn't save the document will surprise you. Print off a copy and ensure your teacher or head of sixth form checks it for you. Do avoid 'cheesy' lines and clichés, such as 'I have dreamt of being a psychologist since being a little girl', as these show a lack of imagination and seriousness. Your statement must stand out as the admissions tutor reads hundreds and your statement is your opportunity to say 'I'm here, choose me, I will be an asset to the course and this is why ...' Grab the attention of the reader, spark interest, and show intelligence and commitment in your statement.

Applying for joint honours courses

If you apply for a joint honours course, such as psychology and sociology, your application will be seen by admissions tutors from both departments, each of whom will want to see that you are a serious candidate for their course. By way of some general advice, note the following.

- Always apply what you have studied/read/done to your course.
- Balance the argument for studying both courses.
- Try to link them – can you see why these two are joint honours?
- Make sure you know why you want to study joint honours and not a single honours degree.

Many universities offer very detailed advice about what they are looking for in a personal statement, and some will reject you if your statement does not conform to what they are looking for. Even if you are not going to apply there, the London School of Economics website contains some very useful advice on writing personal statements. Visit: www.lse.ac.uk/study-at-lse/Undergraduate/Prospective-Students/How-to-Apply/Completing-the-UCAS-form/Personal-Statement.

7 | Succeeding in your interview

Universities interview prospective undergraduates because they want to make sure they are admitting people who will last out a three- or four-year course, making the most of life at university and achieving a good degree. Admissions tutors don't want to rely purely on the UCAS form because, let's face it, most students will have had lots of help with the personal statement and your referee will probably say only nice things about you! At interviews university staff can see what you are really like as a person, how enthusiastic you are about studying psychology and how good you are at thinking about questions you have not had a chance to prepare for.

You may not get called for interview at all, since only a few of the universities now conduct formal interviews. Some universities only tend to invite students for interview if the course or admissions tutor has questions about the personal statement that they want to discuss with the candidate (see Chapter 6). However, a number of universities – usually those with the highest ratio of applicants per place – still ask students to attend a formal interview, and others combine open days with more informal meetings.

If you do apply to a university that interviews applicants, don't worry: the interview is a chance for you to demonstrate to the selectors your suitability for the course. It will not be an unpleasant experience, as long as you do your preparation.

Preparation for interviews

Essential preparation includes rereading the personal statement from your UCAS application. This may well form the basis of preliminary questions (which are meant to put you at your ease) – and if it proves to be a mass of fabrications, the interview is doomed from the start!

Prepare to demonstrate your enthusiasm for the subject and your insight into it by reading about the latest research, focusing on what makes a particular study interesting and newsworthy: are the findings unexpected or controversial? What are the practical implications? Were there ethical issues in carrying out such research? Newspapers and news websites will regularly report new research in psychology, so they are an excellent starting point. You can also check the BPS Research Digest via the website (www.bps.org.uk), which summarises recent studies.

Familiarise yourself with the course you are applying for: make sure you understand what the compulsory elements are and what the optional units are. You may already have ideas about which options you would like to take.

If you have done any relevant work experience, make a bullet-point list of what you did, what you saw, whom you met and what you learnt from the experience. If possible, link this to the course content or your future career goals.

However, don't 'over-prepare'; admissions tutors are interested in seeing the real you, not an airbrushed, carefully rehearsed version of you.

On the day, make sure you wear something clean and smart but comfortable. You don't have to dress formally but you should appear to be taking your application seriously. Basically, you need to show some respect for the admissions tutors in your appearance and not look as if you just got back from a festival. After all, it's an important day for them as well as you.

General hints for interviews

While the number of people conducting the interview and the length of time it takes can vary, all interviews are designed to enable those asking the questions to find out as much about the candidate as they can. It is important, therefore, to engage actively with the process (good eye contact and confident body language help) and treat it as a chance to put yourself across rather than as an obstacle course trying to catch you out. Don't worry, almost everyone gets anxious about interviews and your interviewers will make allowances for this. In fact, if you are too relaxed they may conclude that you are not that bothered about a place.

Interviewers are more interested in what you know than in what you don't know. If you are asked something you can't answer, say so. To waffle (or worse, to lie) simply wastes time and lets you down. The interviewers will be considering the quality of thought that goes into your answers; they will not expect you to know everything already.

> **TIP!**
>
> Pauses while you think are perfectly acceptable; don't be afraid to take your time.

It is possible that one, or more, of the interviewers will be your tutor(s) during your time at university. Enthusiasm for, a strong commitment to and a willingness to learn your chosen subject are all extremely important attitudes to convey. The people you meet at interview not only have to judge your academic calibre, but also have to decide whether they would enjoy teaching you for the next three to four years. Try to demonstrate your enthusiasm by mentioning books or articles that you have read, or topics that you enjoyed as part of your AS or A level Psychology course.

> 'I look for some understanding of what psychology actually is (e.g. the scientific study of the human mind and behaviour), together with enthusiasm for the discipline itself, as well as the potential to develop the academic, personal and employability skills required in a graduate.'
>
> Dr K, senior tutor

An ability to think on your feet is vital. Over-rehearsed responses never work: they appear glib and superficial and, no matter how apparently spontaneously they are delivered, they are always detectable. Putting forward an answer step by step, using examples and factual knowledge to reinforce your points, is far more professional, even if you are not completely sure of what you are saying. That said, it is also sensible to admit defeat: knowing you are beaten is a more intelligent thing than mindlessly clinging to the wreckage of a specious case.

It is possible to steer the interview yourself, to some extent. If, for example, you are asked to comment on something you know little about, confidently replacing the question with another related one shows enthusiasm. Don't waste time in silences that are as embarrassing for the panel as for the candidate.

Questions may well be asked about your extra-curricular activities. Again, this is to put you at your ease: your answers should be thorough and enthusiastic, but not too long! Some more specific psychology-related questions are listed below.

HOPE

Use the acronym HOPE to remind yourself of the personal qualities that you should try to display at the interview:

Honesty
Open-mindedness
Preparedness
Enthusiasm.

Specimen interview questions

The first thing to remember is that it is impossible to prepare for *all* the questions that might be asked in an interview. The interviewers will deliberately want to ask questions that make you think on your feet. So you might as well stop worrying about it beforehand! There are a few predictable questions you should be able to answer, however, without a long pause for thought. The list below includes some of the more obvious questions you might be asked as well as a few calculated to get you thinking and talking on the spot.

1. Why have you chosen to study psychology?
2. What first interested you in psychology?
3. What do you understand by the word 'psychology'?
4. What do psychologists do?
5. What would you like to do after graduating?
6. What are the differences between psychology, psychiatry and psychotherapy?
7. What have you done to investigate psychology?
8. Why did you/didn't you choose to study psychology at A level?
9. Have you read any books on psychology?
10. What particular areas of psychology interest you?
11. How do you keep up with current issues in psychology?
12. Tell me about something that is related to psychology that has been in the newspapers recently.
13. New theories in psychology need to be tested: how do psychologists go about testing theories?
14. Give me an example of an experiment that tests a psychological theory.
15. Is it ethical to experiment on human subjects?
16. Describe some of the links between biology and psychology.
17. Why is a knowledge of mathematics important when studying psychology?
18. Who should judge whether someone has a psychological disorder?
19. How do you cope with stress?
20. How do you relax?
21. What are your best/worst qualities?
22. I see from your personal statement that you are interested in (insert topic/interest). Tell me about it.
23. What are you going to do in your gap year?
24. Why are you taking a gap year?
25. Why did you apply here?
26. What do you like about our psychology course?
27. What options will you choose in the second year?
28. Why did you choose a joint honours degree?

29. Do you know why some psychology degrees are awarded a BA and some a BSc?
30. Are psychologists allowed to divulge information given to them in confidence by a patient?
31. Do you think psychometric testing is a valid way of deciding whom to appoint for a particular job?
32. What is synaesthesia?

In addition to these questions, look out for current debates in psychology that may have been in the news. These could very well provide topics for interview questions. Look out for news of research that has social and ethical implications. For example:

- In June 2017, new research showed that half of 'low intensity' CBT clients relapse within 12 months, suggesting a false economy. Does this research raise ethical questions?
- It has been claimed that neuroscience is now being used to market anything from cars to alcoholic drinks; is this a good use of psychological research?
- One aim of publishing research is to make it replicable and yet few studies are ever repeated; should they be, and if so, why?
- 'The psychology of hate groups: what drives someone to join one?', was the title of a news article published in August 2017 (Elizabeth Chuck, NBC News, 16 August 2017). How can psychology be used to tackle real world problems such as hatred?
- Some psychologists advising on the latest edition of the *Diagnostic and Statistical Manual of Mental Disorders* were challenged because they had worked with major drug companies, who could stand to gain by common examples of human experience being classified as disorders. Should these advisers have resigned?

These are the sorts of debates that academic and professional psychologists are involved in, so you might as well start getting used to them now! Please see Chapter 11 for a list of useful online psychology resources.

> *'When talking to prospective psychology students or reading their applications, I look for a sense of intellectual curiosity, and a willingness to question and to learn. For example, if students have read about an interesting piece of psychological research, I'd like to know about it. Even better, I'd like to see students raising questions about the research that demonstrated thoughtful engagement with it.'*
>
> *Dr M, admissions tutor*

Asking questions of your own

At the end of the interview you are normally given a chance to ask questions of your own. If you have none, say that the interview has covered all the queries you had. It is sensible, though, to have one or two questions of a serious kind – about the course, the tuition, etc. – up your sleeve. Don't ask anything that you could, and should, have found answers to in the prospectus. It is also fine, even desirable, to base a question on the interview itself. This marks you out as someone who listens, is curious and who is keen to learn.

Above all, make the interview panel remember you for the right reasons when they go through a list of 20 or more applicants at the end of the day.

The interview itself: general reminders

- Reread your personal statement to anticipate the questions you may be asked.
- Make sure you arrive early.
- Dress comfortably, but show that you are taking the interview seriously: wear smart, clean clothes.
- Make eye contact.
- Be willing to listen as well as talk, and don't be afraid to ask questions if you are unsure of what the interviewer wants.
- Be willing to consider new ideas, if your interview involves discussion of psychology issues.
- Be yourself.
- Above all, be enthusiastic!

8 | Non-standard applications

Although this book focuses mainly on traditional applications where students have done A levels (or IBs or Scottish Highers, etc.), with an application based on them, there are those who apply to study psychology on a BPS-accredited course with a view to changing their occupation. In 2017, 13,730 UCAS applications for psychology were from those aged 21 or over.

Mature students

Mature students (in general, applicants who are over the age of 21) generally fall into three categories:

1. Those with A level (or equivalent) grades that are sufficient for entry onto a psychology degree course, but who have been working or have been involved in other activities since they completed their studies. For these students, all of the advice in the previous chapters is applicable. They would need to apply through UCAS, as previously described. The main difference might be in the 'Employment' section of the application, where more detail will be required, and in the personal statement, which should contain an overview of what the candidate has been doing since he or she sat their school exams.
2. Those who have already studied at university, but in a different subject. For these students, there are a number of options that will depend on why they are looking at a psychology degree. If the eventual aim is to qualify as a Chartered Psychologist, they should take advice from the BPS about their possible options. In some cases, it may be necessary to study psychology at degree level, but it might be possible to undertake further postgraduate training without the need to do this.
3. Those without the necessary qualifications to be accepted onto a degree course. Potential applicants in this position should contact university admissions departments to discuss their individual situation. They may be advised to take A levels (or equivalent), possibly on an accelerated one-year course offered by some sixth-form colleges, or there may be Access or Foundation courses that are more appropriate.

The importance of the personal statement and CV for mature student applications

Although a certain amount of factual information will be available to the selectors through reading the UCAS application (education details, qualifications, employment details, etc.), it is important that they are able to understand fully the route that the mature applicant has taken to get to the point where he or she is applying for psychology courses. As one admissions tutor says: 'What I want to see is a narrative of the events and decisions that led to the application. Why apply now? What have you been doing since you were at school? What caused the change in direction?'

Some of this can be explained in the personal statement. For example:

> 'After I sat my A levels in 2015, I started as an apprentice in a local law firm. However, I soon realised that this was not the right option for me, so I left and started work in a local nursery. At that time I also started to do some voluntary work in a local primary school, listening to children read and helping on trips, and it was this that sparked my interest in educational issues and, in particular, psychology ...'

If you cannot tell the whole story using the UCAS application and personal statement, then put together a CV and send it directly to the admissions departments. They will then attach this to your UCAS application. In order to ensure that they can match up the CV with your application, send the CV after you have been given your application number from UCAS, and quote this in all correspondence with the universities.

The CV should include details of all employment, and should fill in any gaps. For example:

> **June 2016–April 2017: High Fields Preparatory School, Formby, Merseyside**
>
> Volunteer (two mornings a week) – listen to children read, supervise children on school trips.
>
> **September 2015–April 2016: Loveday & Co. Solicitors, Formby, Merseyside**
>
> Legal administration (full-time) – duties included managing client appointments, filing documents, and drafting letters to clients.

Remember: universities welcome mature students, as they value their experiences and their commitment to their subject. They will be only too happy to give you advice or answer any questions you may have in advance of your application.

For over 50 years the Open University (OU) has provided a route for mature students to study for a degree part time through distance learning. This enables people to gain a degree while pursuing a career and/or raising a family. The OU psychology department has been home to many leading researchers and the degree carries BPS accreditation. In the past few years an increasing number of under-25s have signed up for OU courses. This might be an option worth considering, depending on your personal circumstances. The OU is not part of the UCAS system, so you will not need a personal statement or reference, but it is possible to get access to funding as with conventional universities. For more information visit www.open.ac.uk/courses.

International students

Students who are from outside the UK need to apply for psychology courses in the same way as UK students – using the online UCAS application (www.ucas.com). The UCAS website contains a section for international students which describes the process and the deadlines in detail. The 'Education' section of the UCAS application contains drop-down menus of many international qualifications, not just UK exams.

International students can often be at a disadvantage, not because they are applying from overseas but because they or their advisers are not as familiar with what the selectors at UK universities are looking for in a strong application. This affects two sections of the application:

1.   the personal statement
2.   the reference.

The personal statement for international students

The UCAS personal statement needs to focus on the course itself, and what the applicant has done to investigate it. The advice given in Chapter 4 is equally applicable to international students, and should be read carefully. It is important to remember that the student is 'selling' him or herself to the admissions staff by demonstrating suitability for the course, not on personal achievements or qualities.

In some ways, as an international student you could have certain advantages on your side. For instance, you can compare the differences between your own culture and the UK and what this might mean for psychological theories. If you have already been in the UK for some time doing your A levels you can also demonstrate that you are used to living independently away from home.

References

Often, a promising application is rejected because the person providing the reference is unfamiliar with what is required, and the selectors have no choice other than to reject because they are not given enough information. UCAS references need to focus on the following:

- the student's suitability for the course and level of study
- an assessment of the student's academic performance to date (including level of English, if this is not his or her first language)
- how the student will adapt to studying in the UK
- the student's personal qualities.

If you are unsure whether the person who will write your reference fully understands what is required, show them the section on the UCAS website called 'Non-UK advisers'.

Language requirements for international students

Most UK universities require an International English Language Testing System (IELTS) score of 6.5 or 7 to study psychology (with a minimum of 6 or 6.5 in each of the four sub-tests). Other qualifications such as IGCSE (International GCSE) English or PTE Academic (Pearson's English test) are also recognised. You should check carefully what the English language requirements of your chosen universities actually are: you don't want to be in the position of gaining the A level grades to take up an offer, only to fall down on the English requirement. The UK Border Agency (the visa authority) has no specific English requirement itself, but you will need to produce originals of all qualifications required to meet the terms of the offer once your university place is confirmed. If you have studied in the UK already you will be expected to demonstrate progression in your use of English for your university visa application.

> 'Having lived in China for 16 years I witnessed how people ignore psychological problems. Those with mental illness are treated with medicine that does not help their mental problems and the stigma attached to needing psychological treatment prevents them from seeking help from psychologists. Moreover, psychological treatments are unavailable in some undeveloped countries. The apparently inadequate provision in China has stimulated my interest further and it has made me determined to pursue a psychology-related career, possibly as a clinical psychologist.'
>
> Sally

'Recently, I had an opportunity to do some voluntary work at a hospital in South Korea, where I taught English to children suffering from cerebral haemorrhage. This experience gave me an insight into how illness can be related to psychological problems. These children had limited cognitive abilities and struggled with remembering things. I used with them some of the memory strategies I learned in AS Psychology which proved useful to help those children remember words in English. The outcomes of my intervention persuaded me even more of the need to study psychology to learn how I can help people facing cognitive and behavioural problems. My work at the hospital also helped me to develop my team-working and communication skills as I worked in close cooperation with the medical and the care staff. I was briefed regularly by the staff on the patients as well as providing them with feedback from my work with them.'

Jinseo

Visa requirements

If you require a visa to be in the UK and your course is longer than six months, which psychology courses invariably are, then you will need to apply for a Tier 4 General Student Visa. Before you do this you will need a Tier 4 sponsor: an institution that holds a Tier 4 licence, i.e. the university where you plan to study. In order to do this, your university will request various pieces of information from you, including your education transcripts and passport. They will produce a Confirmation of Acceptance of Studies (CAS) letter for you once you have given them all the information and paid a nominated deposit. You will then need to take the CAS letter to the UK embassy in your country in order to obtain a visa for studying. Do not delay in this process, as obtaining a visa can take time, and this will vary from country to country.

Students with disabilities and special educational needs

If a candidate has a health or learning difficulty or disability, there is a specific section on the UCAS application in which to declare this. Under the personal details section, you must indicate the type of disability/ additional needs you have by selecting the most appropriate from the list available. Thesre is also a section where you are able to elaborate and give further details. Most universities require that you register or make an appointment with Student Services in order for them to carry out any assessments that may be necessary. Universities value and accommodate diversity, so lots of help is available. Visit individual university websites for more information.

9 | Results day

You will receive your results through your school or college and you will be able to find out whether you are accepted onto your chosen courses via UCAS Track (see Chapter 5). If you are very anxious, it might be worth keeping an eye on UCAS Track on the morning of results day. Although you won't know your results, you may well know if you have managed to get into university before you get your results!

When you do get your results one of four things will happen.

- You receive confirmation of your place from the university you selected as your firm choice, and accept it.
- You have not met the offer from your firm choice but you will receive confirmation from the university you selected as your insurance choice and accept it.

> **TIP!**
>
> If you have narrowly missed the grades that you need, your firm (or insurance) choice may still be able to accept you if it has places. Contact it as soon as you can.

- You have met and exceeded the offer made by your firm choice and decide to try to swap courses by going through **UCAS Adjustment**.
- You have not met the requirements of any offers and need to go through **UCAS Clearing**.

If you have achieved the grades that meet the offer made by the university you selected as either your firm choice or insurance choice and are happy with this offer, then congratulations! You do not need to do anything. However, if you want to make use of UCAS Adjustment or have not met any offers and need to use UCAS Clearing, then read on.

UCAS Adjustment

If you have met and exceeded the conditional requirements of your firm choice and it has accepted you – therefore converting the conditional offer into an unconditional one – you could potentially swap your place for one on another course that you prefer. The phrase 'met and exceeded' means that if you needed BBB you would have achieved ABB or better. It doesn't necessarily mean that you just got more UCAS points. For example, if you needed BBB and achieved A*BC, then you would have accumulated more UCAS points with A*BC than you would have if you had only achieved BBB. However, you would have still failed to meet one of your grade requirements. In cases like this your eligibility for Adjustment will depend on whether your offer was based on UCAS points or grades.

You will see the option to register for UCAS Adjustment in Track. Don't worry about your original firm choice, as it will still be safe while you are looking for another course. You will only lose it if you confirm that you would like to go elsewhere and the new university/college adds itself to your application – so it is risk free! UCAS Adjustment is entirely optional and most of the competitive courses will be full, but other applicants might have missed their conditions or swapped a course too, so it could be worth seeing what's available. Adjustment is available for five days from results day or from when your Conditional Firm (CF) offer changes to Unconditional Firm (UF) – whichever is the later, up to 31 August.

To find an alternative course you will need to phone the universities yourself. When you call the universities you will need to give them your UCAS personal ID number and explain straight away that you are applying through Adjustment. Be prepared to answer questions about why you really want to study on that course. If they agree to accept you, and you in turn agree to accept them, this will happen during the phone call. The university will then inform UCAS and your status on Track will change. Remember that if you do not find an alternative course that you want, or do not get accepted onto an alternative course, your original firm offer will still stand.

TIP!

Look carefully at your unit grades, as they may be a means of persuasion. For example, if you studied A level Mathematics and performed particularly well on the statistics units you could mention this to show that you are going to be good at statistical analysis of psychological data.

For more information about UCAS Adjustment visit: www.ucas.com/ucas/undergraduate/apply-and-track/results/adjustment---if-you've-done-better-expected.

If you have no offers

If you are not holding any offers there could be several explanations.

- You may have achieved the right grades but not in the right subjects – for example, you achieved AAB with a B in Biology, whereas your offer was for ABB but with an A in Biology.
- The university or UCAS may not have received your results. These are automatically sent by the examination boards to UCAS, but if you sat an exam at a different centre, for example, then this may not have happened.
- The examination system that you sat does not automatically send the results to UCAS – for instance, if you sat overseas qualifications.

In all such cases, contact your firm choice university to discuss this with it. Universities may revise their offer and admit you if they still have places, or if you missed the grade by only a few marks it may ask you to try for a re-mark. Exam boards change the marks in only a few cases, though, and they can go down or up, so don't place all your hopes on this. If you still do not receive an offer from your firm choice university and have not received an offer from your insurance choice university, then call your insurance choice university. If, by the end of this process, you still have no offers, you will need to enter Clearing.

UCAS Clearing

Clearing is the name given to the system in which all remaining course vacancies are advertised on the UCAS website and in national newspapers. In Clearing, you contact the universities directly that have publicised course vacancies and give them your grades and UCAS ID number. If you think that you might need to use the Clearing system it is best to be well prepared because the vacancies are filled very quickly.

Advice for Clearing

- Make sure that you have your UCAS ID number and a copy of your UCAS application ready for results day.
- You need to have access to a telephone that you can use exclusively, as you may need to make a lot of calls over the course of results day.
- You also need to have access to the internet so that you can have the directory of courses available through Clearing on the UCAS website open. This is particularly useful as the website also has the university contact numbers that you will need to call.

- If you do not have access to the internet you can buy a copy of a national newspaper that lists Clearing vacancies on results day, in preparation for when you get your results.
- Think about the option of studying on courses that might not be identical to the one that you originally applied for, but are related. For example, sociology and psychology rather than single honours psychology.
- Be ready for an impromptu telephone interview. The admissions staff may ask why you want to study on the course, and you will need to have a little bit more tact than just saying 'because I didn't get in to the course I really wanted to'. Instead you could say something like 'Even though I didn't get in to my firm or insurance choices I did apply/intend to apply/visit during the open day/know that the course has a good student satisfaction rating in the *Guardian*, etc.'

TIP!

As with Adjustment, look carefully at your unit grades, as they may be a means of persuasion. You should also look to see how close you were to a grade boundary. If you are applying through Clearing for a course that requires BBB and you achieved BBC and your C grade was one mark from a B grade you may be able to use this to argue that you have the academic credibility to justify a place on the course.

If you decide to retake your A levels

If you decide to retake after having accepted a university place, you will need to let UCAS and the university know that you would like to be released by them, as you will be retaking your A levels. Once you have done this you will be free to reapply through UCAS for the following year. It is advisable for you to contact prospective universities, explaining your situation, so that they can tell you if retake students are at a disadvantage; or, if you are reapplying to a university that rejected you on your first application, if there is any point submitting an application again. Full details can be found on the UCAS website.

In September 2015, the A level syllabus changed to a linear model, which means all exams are now at the end of the second year. This is being introduced on a subject by subject basis, with a different group of subjects moving over to the new model each year, with all subjects due to be moved over by September 2018. If you are considering retaking any subjects, do bear in mind for any 'new' A levels that retaking will mean sitting the whole A level again, not just individual units.

Extenuating circumstances

If issues such as illness, family problems or other problems during the examination period affected your grades, make sure that you have written confirmation of this, such as a letter from a doctor, and present it to the Exams Officer at your school/college so that they can apply for special considerations directly to the relevant exam boards. This should be done as soon as possible before or during the exam period. If you are ill in May and think it might affect your exam performance, don't wait until results day to declare this. It also does no harm to write or email the admissions department for your chosen course with the relevant evidence enclosed/attached. It is more likely that it can make concessions then, rather than when it has already made decisions about whom to accept when the results are issued.

When you have your place

Once your place has been confirmed on UCAS Track, you will receive lots of information from the university that you will be attending, either in the post or by email. This can include information on accommodation, reading lists, when you need to arrive at the university, what you need to bring and Freshers' Week. Freshers' Week is an introductory week for new students organised by the student union to welcome you to the university. It can involve social events, presentations by the university's clubs and societies and the chance to meet current students and other new starters. In short, it will be great fun!

10| Fees and funding

Even before you have secured a place at university you will need to think about fees and funding. In this chapter we look at the different fee systems across the UK as well as the funding available. A comprehensive summary can be found in the 'Student finance' section on the UCAS website at: www.ucas.com/ucas/undergraduate/undergraduate-student-finance-and-support.

Tuition fees

Below is an outline of how the tuition fee system currently works.

Student's home region	Location of university or college			
	England	Scotland	Wales	Northern Ireland
England →	Up to £9,250	Up to £9,250	Up to £9,000	Up to £9,250
Scotland →	Up to £9,250	No fee	Up to £9,000	Up to £9,250
Wales →	Up to £9,250	Up to £9,250	Up to £9,000	Up to £9,250
Northern Ireland →	Up to £9,250	Up to £9,250	Up to £9,000	Up to £4,160
EU →	Up to £9,250	No fee	Up to £9,000	Up to £4,160
Non-EU →	Variable	Variable	Variable	Variable

This table is subject to change and can be found on the UCAS website at: www.ucas.com/ucas/undergraduate/finance-and-support/undergraduate-tuition-fees-and-student-loans.

Most of the higher-ranked universities will charge the maximum amount. Details of what each university intends to charge can be found on the university websites, and also on the UCAS website on the Course Search facility. Please do bear in mind that all the figures included in this chapter are correct at the time of going to press, and that universities in England are able to increase tuition fees each year in line with inflation.

Non-EU students

The fees for non-EU students do not have a set upper limit. The fees will depend on the course and the university. For example, at the University of Cambridge an international (non-EU) student reading psychology would pay tuition fees of £29,217 for 2018 entry. Accommodation and food will be extra (see below). Some UK universities have scholarships available for international students. You should go to the 'International' section on the university websites for more details. Many governments and charities offer scholarships for students to allow them to study in the UK. You should contact your local education department to see if it has contact details.

Brexit

Since June 2016 and Britain's vote to leave the European Union, concerns over fees and access to UK universities for EU students have been raised. Fortunately, the UK government released a statement in April 2017 to clarify the arrangements for EU students wishing to study at UK universities. This statement confirmed that all EU students will remain eligible for undergraduate, postgraduate and advanced learner financial support in the academic year 2018/19. This means that those wishing to study at UK universities will continue to have access to student loans and grants and continue to have 'home fee' status, meaning EU students will continue to be charged at the same rate as UK students. This will remain the case even if your course concludes after Britain's exit from the EU. This information is correct for students applying to English universities for 2018 entry. Depending upon the developments and speed of negotiations regarding Brexit, it is paramount therefore that students applying for 2019 entry check the UK government website for further developments.

Maintenance loans

Maintenance grants in England were abolished in July 2015. Students can still apply for grants if they are eligible for certain benefits, such as Disability Living Allowance, or need help with childcare costs.

The student finance package available to students includes a tuition fee loan and a maintenance loan. The loan you receive from the government to cover your tuition fees will be paid directly to the university on your behalf. However, it is important to remember that this covers only the cost of the actual course you will be studying. You will still need to find money to pay for your rent, bills, books, food, drink and any hobbies or interests. Depending where you are, what sort of accommodation you get and how much you will need to travel, you will need around £12,000–£14,000 for living costs. Please look at the NUS website for further advice on this: www.nus.org.uk/en/advice/money-and-funding/average-costs-of-living-and-study.

If you feel that you are going to have difficulty covering your living expenses you could apply for a maintenance loan. You apply for this at the same time as you apply for a tuition fee loan. If you receive a maintenance loan this will be added to any tuition fee loan that you have and together these loans will make up your total student debt. Maintenance loans will be paid directly into your bank account at various points during the academic year, usually near the start of each academic term.

The amount of maintenance loan is income-assessed. There is a guaranteed portion (less than half in fact) available to everyone, but students from lower income households can borrow more on a sliding scale up to the maximum loan available. For the 2017/18 academic year, the maximum loan per year was £8,430 for outside London and £11,002 for London. This will be paid back in the same way as the tuition fee loan, i.e. once you have graduated or finished your studies and are earning over £21,000 per year.

England

If you are an English student and are starting a full-time course, you will be able to apply for one of the following loans, depending on where you study. The sample figures shown below are for the 2017/18 academic year.

Full-time student	Maintenance loan
Living at home	Up to £7,097
Living away from home, outside London	Up to £8,430
Living away from home, in London	Up to £11,002
You spend a year of a UK course studying abroad	Up to £9,654

For more details visit: www.gov.uk/student-finance.

Scotland

If Scottish students attend a Scottish university, they will not be required to pay tuition fees. However, if they study anywhere else in the UK, they will pay up to £9,250. There are different rules in place for help with funding living expenses, and there are certain bursaries available for students from lower income households. The website of the Student Awards Agency Scotland, www.saas.gov.uk, offers further information on fees and student finance available in Scotland.

Wales

If you are a Welsh student and are starting a full-time course, you will be able to apply for one of the following loans, depending on where you study. At the time of going to press, Welsh students will also be entitled to a Welsh Government Learning Grant of up to a maximum of £5,161, provided that their household income is £50,020 or less. The sample figures shown on the following page are for the 2017/18 academic year.

Your living arrangements during term time	Maintenance loan
Living at home	Up to £5,358
Living away from home, outside London	Up to £6,922
Living away from home, in London	Up to £9,697
You spend a year of a UK course studying abroad	Up to £8,253

For more details visit: www.studentfinancewales.co.uk.

Northern Ireland

At the time of going to press, income-assessed maintenance grants will continue to be available to Northern Irish students starting full-time courses. Currently, the maximum level available is £3,475; if your household income is £19,203 or less, you will be able to receive the full amount. If your household income is over £41,065, you will not be entitled to receive a grant. However, all students will be able to apply for one of the following loans, depending on where you study. The sample figures shown below are for the 2017/18 academic year.

Your living arrangements during term time	Maintenance loan
Living at home	Up to £3,750
Living away from home, outside London	Up to £4,840
Living away from home, in London	Up to £6,780
You spend a year of a UK course studying abroad	Up to £5,770

For more details visit: www.studentfinanceni.co.uk.

Paying back the fees and loans

Fees and loans are not repaid until after the student has graduated and has reached an earnings threshold. The current earnings threshold is £21,000 a year. The amount you repay is 9% of any earnings above £21,000. For example, if you earn £28,000 a year, then you pay back 9% of £7,000 (the difference between £28,000 and £21,000), which is just over £12 per week. The repayment will automatically be taken out of your salary via your tax code.

If you live in Scotland or Northern Ireland and you took out a student loan after 2012, you will repay your loan using repayment plan one. Students living in England will usually follow repayment plan two. For further details on repayment plans, see the students loans company website: www.studentloanrepayment.co.uk.

Alternative help with fees and funding

Financial hardship during your study

If you are struggling to cover costs once you have started a course you may be eligible for hardship funding. The following funding pools are available.

- There are different hardship funds available for students in England, depending on the institution. English students should contact their college or university to check whether they will be eligible for extra funding.
- Support Funds (Northern Ireland).
- The Discretionary Fund (Scotland).
- The Financial Contingency Fund (Wales).

Who gets what and how much is decided by individual course providers. You can usually access this by enquiring at your university's student services or student union.

Other forms of sponsorship

Commercial organisations, charitable trusts, educational institutions and government agencies all offer sponsorship, special grants, access funds and scholarships, but these sources of finance are limited and hard to come by. If you are facing financial difficulties, a good place to start looking for information is the college that you are applying to. The UCAS website contains a section on funding, with contact details and links to a number of funding bodies: www.ucas.com/ucas/undergraduate/finance-and-support/additional-funding.

Funding for postgraduate courses

Students at this level are often self-funded or may be assisted by scholarships from universities or from other organisations. Contacting the institution to which you are applying is a good way to begin exploring your options.

Postgraduate loans are available up to £10,000 to help with the cost of the course fees and living costs. This funding is available for both full-time and part-time study.

Studying overseas

More and more UK students are choosing to study overseas, and they can be divided into two main groups:

1. those whose courses at UK universities involve study abroad
2. those who choose to apply to overseas universities, for example, in Europe, the United States, Canada, or even further afield.

If you fall into the first category, you will be funded in the same way as outlined earlier in this chapter. If you fall into the second category the fees will depend on where you are studying and on what course. It is unlikely that you will get a student loan or assistance with funding from within the UK for these courses; but many overseas universities offer scholarships for international students. A good starting point is to look at the Complete University Guide website: www.thecomplete universityguide.co.uk/international/studying-abroad.

11 | Further information

British Psychological Society (BPS)

The British Psychological Society (BPS) is the professional association for psychologists and is incorporated by Royal Charter. A Register of Chartered Psychologists was established in 1987, bringing a more organised and stricter discipline to the profession. Since 2009 professional psychologist titles are regulated by law and have to be registered with the Health and Care Professions Council (see page 16). Chartered Psychologists are bound to an ethical code of conduct which was set up to maintain the standards of psychology as a profession and to protect the public. The register lists members of the Society who have reached a certain standard in education and work experience. It contains their names, qualifications and work addresses. Chartered members can be found on the BPS website (www.bps.org.uk/bpslegacy/lcm).

The register is split into specialist areas such as clinical, criminological and legal, educational, occupational and counselling psychology. This is also reflected in the different divisions and sections of the memberships for each type of psychologist.

To qualify for registration as a Chartered Psychologist you must:

* have achieved at least a 2.ii in an undergraduate Honours degree accredited by the BPS or completed a Society-based qualification
* have completed psychological research to doctoral level OR completed postgraduate training or have experience teaching psychology
* be judged fit to practise psychology without supervision.

Student membership of the BPS is open to everyone studying on a BPS-accredited undergraduate degree or conversion course. Members get the monthly magazine *The Psychologist*, which, as well as articles and reports on a huge range of research, also carries job advertisements.

The BPS holds a directory of voluntary careers speakers who are members willing to go to schools and colleges to talk about careers in psychology. The BPS website also contains a wealth of information about becoming a psychologist.

For further information contact:

The British Psychological Society
St Andrews House
48 Princess Road East
Leicester LE1 7DR
www.bps.org.uk

Higher Education Academy

The Higher Education Academy publishes an excellent guide to employability for psychology graduates. In the words of the HEA: 'This guide provides a psychology specific overview covering such topics as where psychology graduates work within and outside psychology, emerging areas of work, the job market, and includes activities to help you explore interests, skills, preferences and values.'

www.heacademy.ac.uk/resources/detail/subjects/psychology/
Employability-guide-0.

Other useful organisations

The Association for Coaching
Golden Cross House
8 Duncannon Street
London WC2N 4JF
www.associationforcoaching.com

The British Psychological Society Scotland
Contact address as for main BPS
www.bps.org.uk/networks-and-communities/member-microsite/
scottish-branch

The British Psychological Society Northern Ireland
Contact address as for main BPS
www.bps.org.uk/networks-and-communities/member-microsite/
northern-ireland-branch

The Psychological Society of Ireland
Floor 2, Grantham House
Grantham Street
Dublin 8
www.psihq.ie

The British Association of Sport and Exercise Sciences (BASES)
Room 103, Headingley Carnegie Stand
St Michael's Lane
Headingley
Leeds LS6 3BR
www.bases.org.uk

British Society of Criminology
10 Queen Street Place
London EC4R 1BE
www.britsoccrim.org

Chartered Institute of Personnel and Development (CIPD)
151 The Broadway
London SW19 1JQ
www.cipd.co.uk

UK Council for Psychotherapy
2nd Floor
Edward House
2 Wakley Street
London EC1V 7LT
www.psychotherapy.org.uk

Association of Educational Psychologists
4 The Riverside Centre
Frankland Lane
Durham DH1 5TA
www.aep.org.uk

British Association for Counselling and Psychotherapy
15 St John's Business Park
Lutterworth
Leicestershire LE17 4HB
www.bacp.co.uk

General university guides

HEAP: University Degree Course Offers, Brian Heap, Trotman Education

How to Complete Your UCAS Application, MPW Guides/Trotman Education

How to Write a Winning UCAS Personal Statement, Trotman Education

The University Choice Journal, Trotman Education

University Interviews, Trotman Education

Psychology texts

As far as specific psychology textbooks go, any of the introductory texts found in large bookshops are fine. Those relating to social psychology are probably the easiest and most interesting to read if you are new to the subject.

A User's Guide to the Brain, John Ratey, Abacus

A Dictionary of Psychology, Andrew M Colman, OUP

Classic Case Studies in Psychology, Geoff Rolls, Routledge

Emotional Intelligence, Daniel Goleman, Bloomsbury

From the Edge of the Couch, Raj Persaud, Bantam

How the Mind Works, Stephen Pinker, Penguin

Atkinson and Hilgard's Introduction to Psychology, Susan Nolen-Hoeksema, Wadsworth

Madness Explained: Psychosis and Human Nature, Richard P. Bentall, Penguin

Mapping the Mind, Rita Carter, Weidenfeld & Nicolson

Memory, How We Can Use It, Lose It and Can Improve It, David Samuel, Phoenix

Opening Skinner's Box: Great Psychological Experiments of the Twentieth Century, Lauren Slater, Bloomsbury

Penguin Dictionary of Psychology, Allen, Reber and Reber, Penguin

Phobias: Fighting the Fear, Helen Saul, HarperCollins

QI: The Quest for Intelligence, Kevin Warwick, Piatkus

The Essential Difference, Simon Baron-Cohen, Penguin

The Human Mind, Robert Winston, Bantam

The Jigsaw Man, Paul Britton, Corgi

The Lucifer Effect: How Good People Turn Evil, Philip Zimbardo, Rider

The Man Who Mistook His Wife for a Hat, Oliver Sacks, Picador

The Moral Animal: The New Science of Evolutionary Psychology, Robert Wright, Abacus

The Noonday Demon: An Anatomy of Depression, Andrew Solomon, Chatto & Windus

Thinking, Fast and Slow, Daniel Kahneman, Penguin

Tomorrow's People, Susan Greenfield, Penguin

Totem and Taboo, Sigmund Freud, Routledge

Psychologies (magazine available from newsagents)

Useful websites

British Association for Counselling and Psychotherapy: www.bacp.co.uk

ClinPsy: www.clinpsy.org.uk

Health and Care Professions Council (HCPC): www.hpc-uk.org

Higher Education Academy: www.heacademy.ac.uk

Higher Education Careers Services Unit: www.hecsu.ac.uk

MIND: www.mind.org.uk

NHS: www.nhs.uk

NHS (mental health homepage): www.nhs.uk/livewell/mentalhealth

Neuroscience@nature.com: www.nature.com/subjects/neuroscience

Prospects: www.prospects.ac.uk

PsychMinded: www.psychminded.co.uk

Psychology Today: www.psychologytoday.com

The Psychologist (BPS's monthly publication): www.thepsychologist. bps.org.uk

12| Glossary

Behaviourism is an approach to psychology that sees all behaviour as a learned response to the environment.

Clinical and abnormal psychology concerns the definition, symptoms, classification and theories of different forms of mental illness.

Cognitive psychology covers the understanding of mental processes. It includes the study of memory, thinking and problem solving.

Cyberpsychology is an emerging field that studies human interactions with computers, phones and other electronic devices.

Developmental psychology is the study of the process of human intellectual and emotional growth and development from birth to adulthood.

Evolutionary psychology focuses on the adaptive function of innate psychological characteristics and the role they may have played in human evolution.

Maintenance loan is the money that the government will lend you to pay for your living expenses, e.g. rent, food, etc. You will need to repay the loan when you complete your studies and are earning £21,000 or more per year.

Neuropsychology looks at the relationship between the brain and nervous system and mental processes.

Parapsychology is the scientific study of psychic phenomena such as telepathy, spiritualism and extra-sensory perception.

Psychoanalysis is the type of psychotherapy that grew out of the theories and practice of Sigmund Freud.

Psychodynamics is the approach developed by Sigmund Freud and others seeking to understand personality, behaviour and abnormality through the interaction of conscious and unconscious processes.

Psycholinguistics involves the interface between psychology and language, its acquisition and structure.

Psychometrics is the measurement of attributes such as aptitude or personality, using psychological tests.

Psychopathology studies the origins, causes and development of psychological abnormalities and disorders.

Psychosocial relates to explanations based on a combination of social and behavioural factors.

Psychotherapy refers to the treatment of psychological abnormalities and disorders through psychological techniques.

Tuition fees loan is the money that the government will lend you to pay for your tuition fees. This money will not cover your living expenses, e.g. rent, food, etc. You will need to repay the loan when you complete your studies and are earning £21,000 or more per year.

UCAS Adjustment is a service provided by UCAS for students who have met and exceeded the requirements of their accepted firm conditional choice to potentially swap their place for one on another course they prefer without jeopardising their firm choice. For more information see Chapter 9.

UCAS Apply is the online portal through which you apply to university, including your personal statement and reference.

UCAS Clearing is the system through which all remaining course vacancies are advertised on the UCAS website and in national newspapers from July. Clearing is an important alternative for students who do not make the grade on results day. For more information see Chapter 9.

UCAS Extra is a service provided by UCAS for students who are not holding any offers/do not want to accept any offers. Students can apply to courses available through Extra from early May, one course at a time. For more information see Chapter 5.

UCAS Track is the online portal through which you will receive your conditional offers, select which courses you would like to enrol on and find out whether you have got in on results day.

Abbreviations

ADD: Attention Deficit Disorder

ADHD: Attention Deficit Hyperactivity Disorder

ALF: Adult Learning Fund

APA: American Psychological Association

BA: Bachelor of Arts

BPS: British Psychological Society

BSc: Bachelor of Science

CAMHS: Child and Adolescent Mental Health Services

CBT: Cognitive Behaviour Therapy

CUG: The Complete University Guide

EEG: Electroencephalography

EMDR: Eye Movement Desensitisation and Reprocessing

EP: Experimental psychology

EU: European Union

GBC: Graduate Basis for Chartered Membership

HCPC: Health and Care Professions Council

HEA: Higher Education Academy

HECSU: Higher Education Careers Services Unit

MA: Master of Arts

MA SocSci: Master of Social Sciences

MBPsS: Graduate Member of the British Psychological Society

MPhil: Master of Philosophy

MRI: Magnetic resonance imaging

MSc: Master of Science

NHS: National Health Service

NSP: National Scholarship Programme

NUS: National Union of Students

OCD: Obsessive Compulsive Disorder

PEB: Psychology Education Board

PET: Positron emission tomography

PhD: Doctor of Philosophy

PPL: Psychology, Philosophy and Linguistics

PPS: Politics, Psychology and Sociology

PSI: Psychological Society of Ireland

QAA: Quality Assurance Agency

RAE: Research Assessment Exercise

RCP: Royal College of Psychiatry

TQA: Teaching Quality Assessment

UCAS: Universities and Colleges Admissions Service

Titles in the
Getting into series

Written by experts in a clear and concise format, these guides go beyond the official publications to give you practical advice on how to secure a place on the course of your choice.

Helping you get the career you want

Order today from
www.trotman.co.uk